How to Encourage Your Husband

Also from Prescott Publishing

100 Days of Blessing
by Nancy Campbell

Love Your Husband/Love Yourself:
Embracing God's Purpose
for Passion in Marriage
by Jennifer Flanders

How to Encourage Your Husband

Ideas to Revitalize
Your Marriage

Prescott Publishing

Printed in cooperation with Prescott Publishing
http://prescottpublishing.org

How to Encourage Your Husband
Compiled by Nancy Campbell
Copyright © February 2011, *Above Rubies*

Above Rubies is a magazine to bring strength and encouragement
to marriage, motherhood, and family life. Nancy Campbell has
been publishing *Above Rubies* for over 33 years; it goes to over
100 countries of the world. To receive this life-changing magazine,
which is available by donation, go to www.aboverubies.org or
email your address to nancy@aboverubies.org.

To view resources of books, manuals, DVDs, CDs, and music
recordings to encourage you in your high calling, go to the *Book &
Music Store* at www.aboverubies.org

To receive an encouraging weekly email for wives and mothers,
send a blank email to subscribers-on@aboverubies.org

To join Above Rubies on Facebook, go to
http://facebook.com/AboveRubiesUSS
Come in each morning to receive a positive and encouraging word
to help you through your day of mothering and training the next
generation.

To read hundreds of articles on subjects relating to marriage,
motherhood and family life, go to www.aboverubies.org and click
on ARTICLES AND STORIES.

Front cover design by Heidi Kaether
Westfield, Wisconsin, USA
heidi@daddys-little-princess.com

CONTENTS

FOREWORD

In a society that points to individualism, autonomy, and careerism as the path to personal fulfillment for women, it is refreshing to hear a voice extolling the incomparable blessings of marriage and motherhood. For countless young wives and mothers around the globe, that voice of refreshment belongs to Nancy Campbell, who has been graciously dispensing counsel and encouragement for over three decades through her wonderfully inspiring magazine, *Above Rubies*.

Having been an *Above Rubies* reader since the earliest days of my marriage, I have been personally and profoundly impacted by Nancy's message of vision and purpose. While others were questioning my desire to have a large family and my sanity for doing so, she was sending reassurance and resolve straight to my mailbox, along with practical suggestions for pursuing this high calling more effectively.

In this volume, Nancy compiles some of her readers' best tips on how wives can give that same sort of strength and encouragement to their husbands. I hope that as you read and apply these suggestions, your life and marriage will be abundantly blessed.

JENNIFER FLANDERS
Author of *Love Your Husband/ Love Yourself*

INTRODUCTION

There are many times you may long for more encouragement from your husband. Sometimes you think he doesn't even care about you. You long for him to take more notice of you. You wish that he would show more love to you. In fact, you are in a pit of self-pity! You are totally fed up!

I have a secret for you. Don't wait for your husband to show love and encouragement to you. Give up waiting for him to do special things for you.

"Well," you say, "Do I have to put up with this forever?" Maybe. But you can start from your side. Think of ways to show love to *him*. Think of special ideas to surprise *him*. Make an effort to say, "I love you" as often as you can. Think of special things to say to him that will make him feel amazing. Honor him. Respect him. Make his life exciting.

"But I can't think of anything to encourage him about," you answer. Take some time to consider it. There must be something you can think of or you wouldn't have married him. Ask God to bring that to your mind. And let me tell you, you won't feel like doing it. You'll have to do it by faith. You'll have to do it because it is the right thing to do. Forget your feelings. Just do it!

"This is all so one-sided," you argue. Yes, it will start out like that. But wait! As you do loving things, you will become more loving, and you will fall more and more in love with your husband. As you say loving things, you will become sweeter and lovelier. As you think about how you can bless him, you will see more and more of his good points. You will change. And gradually he will change, too. He will not be able to resist your love. No man can resist the genuine charms and love of his wife.

Song of Songs 7:6 and13 tell us to bless our husband with charms that are *"both new and old."* We can become such terribly boring wives. Are you still in the "old" rut? Try a "new" road! Spice up your marriage and spend some time thinking about some new ways to delight your husband. God intends you to have fun together.

Revolutionize your marriage. Boot boredom out the door! Open the door to love and excitement. You will be amazed at what will happen.

Husbands are desperate for love and encouragement. Maybe your husband didn't receive all the encouragement he needed as a child. Maybe your husband is still lacking and his confidence tank is not yet filled up. You can fill up that lack in your husband. You'll be amazed at what happens to him when he gets filled up. Proverbs 12:25 says, *"A word of encouragement does wonders."* Look out! When you start encouraging your husband, wonders will happen!

Keep reading. The following are many ideas that *Above Rubies* readers have sent to me. Be inspired to start a new way of living in your marriage as you read all these wonderful ideas. But don't stop with this book. Take time to think of new, creative ones yourself.

NANCY CAMPBELL
Primm Springs, Tennessee, USA

Chapter 1

TOP OF THE LIST—RESPECT YOUR HUSBAND!

"Let each man of you (without exception) love his wife as (being in a sense) his very own self; and let the wife see that she respects and reverences her husband—that she notices him, regards him, honors him, prefers him, venerates and esteems him; and that she defers to him, praises him, and loves and admires him exceedingly."

- Ephesians 5:33, Amplified

HIGH ON THE LIST!

Recently I sat down before the children were out of bed and handwrote a letter to my darling husband. I told him how much I respected him and gave him specific examples. When I finished the letter, I mailed it to his work address. Husbands desire many things, but respect is high on the list. After many years of marriage, I desire him to know that my respect is deeper, my love grander, and my desire multiplied over the years—not only in words, but in a handwritten letter.

TANYA ROBINSON
Marietta, Ohio, USA
wearealladopted@gmail.com

HELP HIM WALK TALL!

Many men in today's generation struggle to find how to take their role as head of their family. So few have grown up in a household where they saw it working firsthand. I believe that one of the greatest ways to encourage a husband is to help him to take up his position as the head. It takes a lot of humbleness, and there have been many times I have failed. But the times I get it right are the times I see my husband walking tall and ready to take on the world. Steve has a lot more confidence when he knows that he has a support team behind him that is not going to argue with the direction he chooses for his family.

Before we had children I was a nurse and was used to "taking charge." It has taken a lot of work to learn to "die to self" and let someone else have charge of situations. I think I will be working on this for a lifetime. I know that it is worth my efforts, because it is only when things are in order at home that a husband can rise up and be all that God wants him to be.

ANNIE BARNES
Morningside, Queensland, Australia
annie@stevebarnes.id.au

IT'S HOW THEY FEEL LOVED!

Lately, I've been trying to tell my husband that I respect him and appreciate his hard work for us. When I send e-mails, I sign them, "All my RESPECT and love," and not just love! Men love to be respected. It's their way of feeling loved.

MARGE DENSLEY
Montgomery, New York, USA
mdensley@frontiernet.net

DO THE THINGS HE LIKES

I regularly tell my husband how much I RESPECT him. I find this blesses him even more than telling him how much I love him. Men thrive on being respected. My husband is in the trucking industry where there is not much in the way of respect, and so he is very encouraged by my respect.

Another way to encourage our husbands is to do the things they like! For example, I am from New York, and my husband is from Tennessee. He loves to drink Southern sweet tea. I didn't even know what it was when I met him! I learned how to make it especially for him, even though I don't particularly care for it myself. I also learned how to make some of his favorite dishes, maybe not as well as his mom, but I try!

We also need to be available to our husbands in bed. I do not ever say, "I'm not in the mood."

Recently I called my husband to ask, "Jake, is there another way I can encourage you?" I was thrilled to hear, "Wow, Sarah, I can't think of anything else you can do to make me happier or more fulfilled." *Thank you, Jesus!* Then he said, "You can scoop the litter box!"

SARAH RAGEN
Deltona Florida, USA
sarahrr123@earthlink.net

HE WANTS MORE!

Some time ago, a lady called to change her address and in the course of conversation mentioned a book by Dr. Emerson Eggerichs called *Love and Respect*. I wrote it on a bit of paper, popped it in the drawer, and promptly forgot about it. Not long after, Bill and I had a few words, nothing major to be sure, but we were definitely frustrated with each other.

"But, Bill, you know I love you." I stated my case.

"Yes, Val, I know you love me," Bill answered.

"And you know I do my best to be submissive to you."

"Yes, Val, I know you are submissive," he confirmed.

"You also know I'm forgiving," I continued.

"Yes, Val, I know you are forgiving," he patiently replied.

"Well then, isn't that enough? What else do you want of me?" I wanted to know.

"I don't know, Val, but it isn't enough," Bill replied quietly.

"So you're telling me that love, submission, and forgiveness are not enough?" I demanded to know.

"Yes, Val, that's what I'm telling you."

"And you can't tell me what this something is?"

"No, I can't, Val. I just know I want it."

I marched off furiously. What else does he want from me?" I muttered to myself. "I don't have any more to give." In my frustration I felt that most men would be grateful for those three elements in their marriage, but not my husband. No, he wants MORE! I cried out to God for help, feeling it was so unjust.

Rummaging through a drawer I came across the name of the book the lady had given me. I checked out the Internet, ordered, and to my surprise, it arrived within two or three days. Dropping everything, I sat down to read. Within the first chapter I knew the missing ingredient in our marriage. It was *Respect*. I had obviously answered Bill in a disrespectful way that day we were frustrated with one another.

I decided to test the theory explained in the book. Approaching Bill, who was working out in his shed, I took care to tell him how I really respected him in a certain area. Right before my eyes his whole demeanour softened. He smiled. *It can't be that easy,* I thought. *I'll leave it for a couple of hours and try again.* Two hours later I told Bill how I respected him on yet another aspect of his character. Once again he seemed to grow in stature. I realised I had won his heart. He was like putty in my hands.

Respect is what a husband longs for, even though he may not be able to put his finger on it.

VAL STARES
Beaudesert, Queensland, Australia
valstares@aboverubies.org.au
Val is the Director of *Above Rubies* in Australia

LET HIM BE THE MAN!

The greatest way I encourage my husband is to let him "be the man!" Freeing our marriage from criticism and also my attempts to dominate and control has given him the freedom to be the godly man he is becoming. I ask his opinion and value his advice on everything—from our homeschool schedule and materials to my wardrobe and Biblical issues. I listen to him talk about work without trying to interject my thoughts. I try not to waste his precious home time complaining about my tough day. If he calls to ask how our day is going, I always tell him it's great so he doesn't dread coming home to chaos.

We try to pick up the clutter before he comes home. When he arrives home, we stop what we're doing to run and hug him and let him know we're glad he's home. During our family prayers I pray out loud for him for his work or travel. The children have begun doing the same, which lets him know we love him and care about what goes on when he's busy providing for us.

The fruit of our efforts is evident. He adores our family and can't wait to get home to be with us. Even at times when he could be enjoying himself, guilt-free at a social work function, he has been known to excuse himself early because he wants to kiss his children goodnight before they fall asleep. He reads Bible stories to our children at night. Most importantly, he is going deeper into the Bible with the goal of becoming a true Christ-follower—and he is taking us all with him.

BECKY LEFTWICH
Carrollton, Georgia, USA
rebeccaleftwich@bellsouth.net

I RESPECT YOU!

When my husband came to me and told me I never built him up, I thought, "That's impossible! I think those things all the time!" And I did; only I didn't verbalize them. I decided to verbalize my thoughts, "I respect you so much for...." Or "God must be so pleased with you for your obedience to...." Of course, there are the little, seemingly silly things, "You are so strong!" Or, "You can fix anything." Watch him grin when you say these things.

HEATHER STROUSE

HE'S NOT A CHILD

I have found that the best way to encourage my husband is not to be his mother. He is not a child and should not be treated as such.

The husband is the head of the home and should not be scolded or nagged by his wife.

Unfortunately, I am still reaping the results of the years I didn't follow this advice. My husband thanks me for not scolding him when he is late, and I can tell he is nervous coming into the house. How sad I did this to him before! Our marriage is so much better since I have made efforts to change my negative behavior. My husband notices and tells me how much he appreciates me. He has always put me first, done his best to take care of me and help me at home, but now I think he enjoys doing it so much more.

LINDA CRAWFORD
Lancaster, Kentucky, USA
Peanut25987@cs.com

PRACTICAL WAYS

I find I can show my husband respect, not only in word, but in practical ways.

My husband takes his place at the head of the dinner table each meal. The children do not need to be given a Bible lesson to teach them that Daddy is the head of the home. They see it before their eyes every day as he sits at the head of the table.

We have two chairs between our kitchen and dining room, one for my husband and one for me. Colin's is the most comfortable and I often sit in it, but if he walks in the room, I immediately vacate the chair to show respect to him. Anyone else sitting in the family who sits in his chair will also get up immediately he comes into the room.

Colin also has his chair in the lounge by the fire. Anyone sitting in this chair will get up immediately if he comes to sit in it.

Even in these little ways, I can show honor to him.

NANCY CAMPBELL

Chapter 2

VERBALIZE—YOUR WORDS HAVE POWER!

YOU MAKE MY DAY!

Each time we meet you always say
Some word of praise that makes my day,
You see some hidden, struggling trait,
Encourage it and make it great.
Tight-fisted little buds of good
Bloom large because you said they would.

A glad, mad music in me sings;
My soul sprouts tiny flaming wings,
My day takes on a brand new zest,
Your gift of praising brings my best,
Revives my spirit, flings it high;
For God loves praise, and so do I.

IN FRONT OF THE CHILDREN

I love to talk highly of my husband to others when he is present—and even when he is not. I used to be a nagging wife but saw the damage I was doing to our children. Now I make it a point to praise my husband on a regular basis in front of my children, and to my children. I want them to know how blessed they are to have a father who allows me to stay home with them and homeschool them, who loves the Lord and sows Christ's love in to our lives.

DEBORAH GILCREASE
Tyler, Texas, USA
chefdebg@gmail.com

THE SHABBAT MEAL

Although I try to encourage my husband daily, there is one time each week when I formally encourage my husband. This is at our weekly Shabbat meal. At this meal it is traditional for the husband to read Proverbs 31 and then bless and encourage his wife. I then have the opportunity to respond. I often read Psalm 112 before I bless my husband. This is one of the most beautiful moments of our week where we encourage one another, in front of the family and visitors.

Because we do it every week, we have to think of new things to say. It gets rather boring to say the same thing week after week! This makes me take time to think about my husband and to think of special things that have endeared him to me during the previous week. This special meal is a beautiful way to keep marriages together.

NANCY CAMPBELL

Note: If you would like to read more about how to prepare a Shabbat meal, go to www.aboverubies.org, click on *Articles and Stores*, and then the following posts, *The Preparation Day* and *The Shabbat Meal*. You may also like to read *Every Meal a Love Affair* of how a marriage was saved through the Shabbat Meal.

MARRIAGE CHANGING WORDS

When I want to see my husband's face glow I tell him, "Thank you." His response is always a little smile and a questioning look on his face. "For what?" he'll ask. I give him an answer such as…

- *"For the three pairs of wet panties from our potty-training two-year old."*

- *"For the joy of hearing our six-year-old little daughter read her first words today."*
- *"For the total excitement of watching our son kick a goal in the game on Saturday."*
- *"For this beautiful home that keeps me warm while I snuggle and nurse yet another sleepy baby."*
- *"For working so hard today and coming home tonight."*
- *"For your prayers over me and our children on your lunch break. Honey, I could go on and on. I have everything I have ever wanted right here, and I thank you that you let me enjoy being what God intended me to be."*

He looks at me and says, "Really?" I nod and assure him that I mean it. Really!

Our home is humble. The dishwasher, oven and stove are really old. Our cabinet doors are coming apart. The windows are not "energy efficient" because they let in whatever temperature we are trying to keep out! Everything my children and I wear comes from someone else's closet to ours. But, my husband knows I am content. He knows I am thankful for everything I have—mostly for him and our children. He knows he is the king of this earthly castle, and he is respected and adored. And despite what others called a "hopeless marriage," we now have a marriage made in heaven. Saying "Thank you" has made a difference!

BRANDI GUERRERO
Montevallo, Alabama, USA
bdguerrero75@yahoo.com

THANK YOU FOR WORRYING

Tony and I have recently had some very stressful financial struggles. One day he was particularly frustrated and crabby toward me and the children. He was sitting in the office doing the bills, and I came up to him and gave him a hug and said, "Thank you for worrying about the money. I know it stresses you out, but I am glad you care about us enough to want to make things better." Later, out of the blue, he said to me, "Thank you for saying that earlier, it meant a lot to me."

ELISSA BASTINELLI
Hillsboro, Oregon, USA
buwissa@hotmail.com

BEAUTIFUL WORDS IN THE DARK

After a few years of trial and error, I discovered that affirming words are the most important way to express love to my husband. This could only be God's idea since I have very little brain-to-mouth filter. I think out loud and change my mind in the process while my husband's words are always measured. My husband has always enjoyed the sound of my voice—it's soothing to him. At the end of the day as we lay in the dark, I say a quick prayer and speak beautiful words over him. I speak over him all the things I appreciate he has done, or is doing, how I love his character, or specific ways he is a great husband and father. Most of the time, my lovely words send him to sleep. I know that it is not from boredom—it's a peace and comfort that his God-given bride provides through encouraging words.

LEAH SMITH

THE LUCKIEST WOMAN IN THE WORLD

During our supper meal together I start out by saying, "I'm the luckiest woman in the world. I'm so glad you are faithful go to work every day to provide for us." The children then chime in with their encouraging words such as, "You are so strong, Daddy...

some men are sick and skinny!" and so on. They think of different things each time! It is so wonderful to see his smile grow and grow as each child chimes in with their praise. It has a double effect on him when I praise him in front of others, and even more so when he grows in stature in the children's eyes.

KELLY MIDKIFF
Holden, Missouri USA
ahappywife@hotmail.com

CHEER HIM ON!

Over a year or so ago my husband cut off his left thumb. I try to point out to him the many things that he does with one thumb (like plumbing for instance) that a lot of men with two thumbs cannot do. I think this encourages him to see how far he has come in his recovery. When he feels frustrated or discouraged, it is good for him to hear me say that, in my eyes, he is an overcomer!

BECKY MESSER
Missionaries in San-Pedro, Cote d'Ivoire, West Africa. When in USA they live in Winston-Salem, North Carolina, USA
andymesser@aviso.ci

HIS SMILE RETURNED

Early in our marriage, my husband and I both purposed that he would be the breadwinner and I would not pursue a "career" outside of the home. However, the arrival of our first child with special health problems put a new burden on my husband as he strived to be the best provider he knew how to be. I saw the lines around his young eyes and his stooped shoulders, The Lord convicted me that I was guilty of worrying "out loud." My spoken confessions of fears and worries about the money, the medical bills, etc. compounded the burden my husband already carried.

The Lord showed me that to *"do my husband good, and not evil"* (Proverbs 31:12), required a resolute CHOICE to speak words of faith, gratefulness, and hope for the future. I asked my husband to forgive me for my complaining. I humbly told him I had changed my mind about pursuing government aid for our son's medical bills, and said, "I know God is big enough to take care of this." And God did. Both our hearts grew larger in faith. I daily tried to speak words of faith in God's provisions. I would say, "You are such a faithful provider, honey. I know God is bigger than any need we have. I am happy with *whatever* He provides, through *your* income." His smile returned and his shoulders squared up again.

I once asked him about the tithe for church. When he wondered out loud if we could afford to tithe or if God really expected that of *us,* I sweetly suggested he put God to the test, as God offers in Malachi. My husband did, and within a month, God moved him into a different job with double the income. He has tithed every payday since then, teaches our children to tithe, and exhorts others on the topic. 1 Peter 3:8-9 tells me that I am called to *"be a blessing and to inherit a blessing"* by speaking words of blessing.

KAREN McDANIEL
Montezuma, Indiana, USA
fortressfellowship@yahoo.com

JUST PENDING

When my husband, Josh is discouraged because our income is lower than normal (he's a building contractor, so it fluctuates!) I remind him that we aren't "poor," even if we have NO money in our bank account. We are just "pending." He LOVES that statement, and it always brings a smile! It takes a lot of the pressure off him as the provider.

KIM BENNETT
Smithsburg, Maryland, USA
Kkimmikim@aol.com

A CROWN OR A CANCER

Do you find yourself with a knife for a tongue? Has this weapon ever injured your husband's spirit? Or am I the only one that this has happened to? Let me share how God worked in my life.

It started out like a normal afternoon after my husband arrived home from work. I was happy to serve him a drink when he arrived and helped him with his things. I listened to him talk about his day. Then, after a favor I asked him to do and he did wrongly, I snapped. Anger welled up inside me. It started with frustration, then sarcasm, then yelling. At the climax of my temper fit, I grabbed one of his favorite magazines, tore it apart and then, even worse, ran it through our paper shredder!

"Maybe NOW you'll listen!" I cried with one last stab. He was so angry and just left me standing there. Am I proud to share this? No. I am ashamed of such dishonoring, disrespectful behavior! For the next hour my anger seethed, but then images of my husband's shocked face convicted me. I had really hurt him. I fell to my knees, engulfed in broken sadness and conviction. I cried out to the Lord to forgive me for my actions, for letting my anger rear its ugly head, and for lashing out the way I did. I asked God to remove this spirit of anger from me and to create in me a pure heart. With each tear I prayed for mercy, strength, renewal, and a new mouth. All that I asked for, He gave me.

I went to my husband. He saw me walk in and braced for another verbal battle. His face was hard and his arms crossed. What heartbreak that the "love of my life" had become so used to my abuse. I know he expected me to go for a second round, start dredging his mistake up all over again and then hammer it in with another round of cutting words. Instead, I lowered myself before him and cried. I told him that I was sorry for everything I had said and done. I told him that I loved him and appreciated everything he does for me. I asked for a second chance to show him the respect and love he deserves. I shared with him how God had taken these things from me and cleansed my heart.

He was so overwhelmed by this unexpected turn that he burst into tears himself. He showered me with hugs and kisses, telling me he still loved me. To hear him forgive me was music to my ears. I am so grateful.

Now, instead of complaining about his work boots left out, I choose to help him remove them and give his tired feet a rub. Instead of giving him a list of things to take care of after work, I leave a note listing all the things I love about him. I am determined to love my husband, honor him, and treat him like the gift that he is. I will be a crown to him instead of cancer to his bones. Every time I look at my shredder, I am reminded that I have a choice. I can build up and create an atmosphere of peace, blessing and love, or I can shred and destroy.

ANGEL RODRIGUEZ
San Antonio, Texas, USA
blessedwifenmom@gmail.com

SPEAKER PHONE

I like to call my husband at work during the day and put the children and myself on speaker phone. We all talk to him and he hears the children's giggles. Even the baby has a chance to coo at Daddy! He says it puts the hectic pace of work into perspective when he hears our voices.

KRISTY SMITH
San Antonio, Texas, USA
smiths4jesus7@att.net

LEAVE A VOICE MAIL

When my husband is feeling stressed or having a rough time at work, I call his office and leave him a voice mail. I make sure to call right after he leaves the house. When he gets to work, it's on his voice mail. I tell him how much I respect him and his commitment to provide for our family, how much I appreciate all the hard work he does for us, and how proud I am of him for sticking with it even when it is very difficult. He saves the message and listens to it again when he needs a boost!

GINA McINTOSH
Fort Collins, Colorado, USA
ginamcintosh@yahoo.com

MISSED CALLS

When my husband and I were first married, he told me that "it's the little things that count." What *little things* could I do to make sure he felt appreciated, respected, and treasured? At that time, I was blessed to have him home with me during the day as he was beginning a distance education program. He was only away a few hours in the evening while he went to a part-time job. I missed him so much even during those few hours that I would call his cell phone just in case I could catch him on a break. He could not hear my calls because of where he was working but his phone displayed another "missed call" from home. Checking his phone on the way home he would be thrilled to see how many times I had called. He knew I was thinking of him.

Soon our circumstances changed and he returned to fulltime work. When he first started his new job, he told me he'd put his phone on silent, but I could still call him while he was working. Throughout the day, as I go from task to task, I keep the phone tucked in my apron or on the counter beside me. Every once in a while I give him a call just to let him know I care. My missed calls are *little things* that make his day!

REBECCA MCKAY
Prince George, British Columbia, Canada
bandb@ncol.com

LIGHTING HIS FIRE

Telling my husband how proud I am of him and how much I respect him does wonders for him. His face lights up. His whole demeanor changes. He's like a brand new man, willing to accomplish anything for his family.

KARIN HANUS
Janesville, Wisconsin, USA
nirak1025@aol.com

IT'S HARD TO BE UPSET

I constantly tell my husband what he's doing right and how much I appreciate all he does for our family, even if it's something as simple as him helping around the house or providing financially for us. I constantly tell him he is a wonderful example of Christ's love for the church as he shows me unconditional love. By trying to think of something wonderful about my husband in the daily routine of life, it helps to remind me how great he really is and enables me to focus on his positive qualities. It's awfully hard to be upset at him when I'm constantly thinking of all of the wonderful things he does!

SARAH O'REILLY
Indianapolis, Indiana, USA
saraheoreilly@yahoo.com

TELL THE WORLD

I love to complement my husband, especially in front of him when I tell my friends the wonderful things he does for me. I like to brag what a blessing it is for me that he works hard so I can stay at home, how sweet he is, and how he is the best at everything.

KELLIE BRADLEY

THREE LITTLE WORDS

The comforting smells of supper fill our kitchen as the clock on the wall strikes 4 pm. The home is cleaned and the children washed and ready. Soon my husband will arrive, and I want everything to be perfect. My heart skips with anticipation as I envision him coming home, his cheery smile bringing warmth to our home as he looks with delight at his precious children. Then holding me and looking tenderly into each other's eyes we share our day with each other.

The tires of my husband's truck on the carport awaken me from my daydream. The children rush to surround him with hugs but stop short at his sad countenance. "Hi honey," he offers from the threshold, "What's for supper?" I walk over to give him a hug.

"Maybe this will help," I think. His discouragement and sadness sink deep into my soul as he returns my embrace with a pat on the shoulder and a duty peck of a kiss. "I'm beat," he mumbles as he wanders into the living room and sinks into his favorite chair. This was a description of my married life for many years until Nancy shared with me a key element that was missing. This opened the door to my husband's heart and revolutionized our lives.

Our lives as a married couple can be described as difficult, at best. We were young and easily influenced. Others dated, so we did. Others married, so we did. Not much of a love story. I also came to realize that, as a Christian, I had married out of God's will and I became bitter and angry with myself. Then I became judgmental toward my husband and compared him to other "spiritual" men both in my mind and in front of him. When children arrived on the scene, I happily turned my attention and love toward them. Basically, I shut my husband out.

God soon convicted me, and I repented to Him and my husband. What was done was done, no matter what. I had promised the Lord to stay with this man "till death do us part." I was determined to keep that promise. I purposed in my heart to be the best wife and mother ever. I read all of the books and put them into practice. I learned to make good healthy meals on a shoestring; I carefully stayed within budget, and submissively cared for my husband.

As the seeds I had planted early in our marriage began to sprout in my husband's heart, they blossomed into the fruit of sadness and discouragement. At times, he was overwhelmed. I doubled my efforts to please him and make him happy. I canceled all afternoon appointments in order to stay home and minister to my husband, I waited on him so he could rest in the afternoons, and did my best to maintain a happy atmosphere in the home, but still we drifted apart. Love is a verb, I was told; so why didn't doing all of these things make him love me? Why was he so sad?

Love was an emotion that was foreign to me as a wife, so I hoped it would come through the performance of loving duties. But it didn't. I thought this was how it would always be and resolved myself to my dilemma. I would live with an empty heart and so would my husband—until death parted us. After all, I reasoned, how could I ever love someone who didn't love me? Then I met Nancy Campbell. After an exhausting and encouraging *Above Rubies* Ladies' Retreat, it was my turn to spend time with her as I transported her to the nearby airport.

My companion and I pelted her with questions concerning marriage, children, cooking, etc., while a very tired Nancy patiently answered each one. Then, just before she left on the plane she gave the key for which I had long searched. "Tell him," she encouraged, "tell him you love him." She must have read into the blank stare I gave her as she continued. "You don't have to feel anything right now. Prophesy out loud to him that you love him. The feelings will come later." That was a shock to me. I thought the feelings had to come first.

The next morning as I shuffled to make my husband's morning coffee, Nancy's words rang in my head. "Tell him." The battle raged within. I had allowed Satan to rule in this area, and he wasn't going to give up so easily. Surely it can't be that hard to say those simple words, I reasoned. Doubts crept in. I prayed silently for strength as my husband drank his coffee. I peered into his tired eyes that revealed his hurting heart. As he rose to leave I embraced him tenderly, kissed him as usual, and then I did it. The words "I love you" spilled from my lips!

I waited for his response. Not exactly what I expected. He looked at me as if he'd seen a ghost and quickly retreated out of the house for work. I was a little disappointed, but the Lord revealed to me that deep wounds heal best when they heal slowly from the inside out. I diligently repeated those three words every day, and as the days turned to weeks I began to notice a change in my husband.

Harsh words were replaced with compassionate ones, empty looks changed to affectionate gazes, and half-hearted taps on the shoulder turned into tender embraces.

Emotions stirred in my heart, as well, and love filled me. It pushed out sadness, discontent, fear, and worry. I was able to really pray for the needs of my husband as never before—prayers of encouragement and strength for his day, prayers for wisdom in leading our family and from protection from harm on the job. I also prayed against doubts and fears that would try to distract him and pull him down and drain him emotionally. Satan lost his grip on our marriage, and the Lord began taking control.

Then one day it happened. As we lay down for the night, my husband's strong arm resting comfortably under my head, I leaned over and, with a gentle kiss, whispered again, "I love you." His arms embraced me so tenderly and lovingly. He cleared his throat and replied, "I love you, too." A tear crept from the corner of my eye and trickled down my cheek. The miracle had happened. My husband and I were in love and still are, and it all started with those three little words, "I love you."

Now, it's 4 pm. The wonderful aroma of supper fills our home and the children and I wait in anticipation for the love of my life to arrive. My excitement mounts as the door begins to open... because today I know my dream of a happy homecoming has become a reality.

ANGELA DECOTEAU
St. Amant, Louisiana, USA
decotec@eatel.net

I'M HIS CHEERLEADER!

Are you your husband's cheerleader? I am. And no, I did not start out that way. Regretfully, it wasn't until many years into my marriage that I became aware of God's design for a wife to be a helpmeet to her husband. After I became more educated on the subject, I made it my job to fill that role to the best of my ability. I haven't become perfect, but I keep striving towards the goal.

One way I do this is to constantly reaffirm him. I speak words to him like, "You handled that so wonderfully" or "You are such a good daddy." I do this, not because he has asked me to, or because he is weak and needs me to, but because I see how it makes him feel. He smiles and thanks me. And although he'd never admit it aloud, it makes him proud and confident. Men are starving for their wife's affirmation.

One of my brothers enjoys teasing my husband. One day he and I were having a discussion and I piped up, "I bet Brian could do that. He's very good with projects of that sort." My brother rolled his eyes and said, "What, are you his cheerleader?"

"Yes, I am!" I replied. My brother laughed it off. But, unknown to me, my husband had come in on the tail end of the conversation and smiled. It is wonderful to give your husband praise—even more so in front of others.

NICOLE STEINC
Lake Wales, Florida, USA
brianandnicole65@msn.com

SING HIM A SONG

My husband, Jim, is in sales which has its ups and downs, much like a roller coaster. I started to sing to my husband when he closed a sale, "I'm proud of you, I'm proud of you, Oh, yes, I'm so proud of you. Boop, Boop, Dee, Do!" Much to my surprise, it really spurred him on. He tries his hardest to get as many sales each day as he can, so he can call and hear me sing his reward. I know this really showed him how much I appreciate him going out and working hard for our family.

ANGI MARTIN

SWEET WORDS

My husband loves me to speak sweetly to him. If I start to get on my "high horse," he will say to me, "Nancy, you've got to be sweet to me." Oh my! I don't have a chance to get harsh! Sweet words endear us to our husband. Speaking to his bride in Song of Songs 4:11, Solomon says, *"Thy lips, O my spouse, drop as the honeycomb: honey and milk are under thy tongue."* What drips from the honeycomb? Sweetness! What kinds of words drip from your tongue to your husband? You will bless your husband when you drip sweet words, soft words, encouraging words, cheerful words, positive words, helpful words, supportive words, kind words, wise words, forgiving words, loving words, pleasant words and life-giving words.

A friend shared this quote with me: "People turn their best side out: they are delightful in company, but snarly at home. There they give vent to their dissatisfaction, their temper, their grouch. They are scent-bottles abroad, vinegar-bottles at home... To be a Christian at home one must learn to 'keep sweet.'"

Proverbs 15:1 says, *"A gentle answer turns away wrath."* (NASB) And here is another challenge from Song of Songs 4:3, *"Thy lips a line of scarlet, guardians of that sweet utterance."* (Knox translation) Do our lips guard the harsh and nasty words that can fall from our lips? What a lot of heartache we would save if we would only speak gentle words. Shakespeare's famous words are apt for us: "Her voice was ever soft, gentle and low, an excellent thing in woman."

NANCY CAMPBELL

Chapter 3

LOVE NOTES

Do it now!

If with pleasure you are viewing any work a man is doing,
If you like him or you love him, tell him now;
Don't withhold your approbation
till the parson makes oration
And he lies with snowy lilies on his brow;
No matter how you shout it he won't really care about it;
He won't know how many teardrops you have shed;
If you think some praise is due him
now's the time to slip it to him,
For he cannot read his tombstone when he's dead.

More than fame and more than money
is the comment kind and sunny
And the hearty, warm approval of a friend.
For it gives to life a savor,
and it makes you stronger, braver,
And it gives you heart and spirit to the end;
If he earns your praise-bestow it;
if you like him let him know it;
Let the words of true encouragement be said;
Do not wait till life is over and he's underneath the clover;
For he cannot read his tombstone when he's dead.

- Berton Braley

CHARACTER QUALITIES

I have made a habit of leaving little notes for my husband to find. Sometimes it is a list of character qualities I admire in him, or "10 reasons why I love you", or "10 things that make you a great dad!"

BENITA WICKS
Clayton, Delaware, USA
benitawicks_5@msn.com

PHYSICAL ADORATION

I am challenged by the conversation recorded in Song of Songs 5:9. Her friends ask her, *"How is your beloved better than others?"* She answers with no less than ten praises about her man's physical glory. She did not even touch any of his character qualities! I realized that this is a valid response that we should all be able to answer about our husbands! I think that we often forget, or minimize the need to praise our men physically. Men, just as much, or more so, need to know how desirable we find them! This encourages them immensely, and helps them feel self-confident and virile!

I decided that day that I would give this a most concerted effort. I texted my husband at work with these words, "I think you are drop dead gorgeous. I love your eyes, your face with all of its character and your smile. I love your laugh, your strength and your playfulness with the children. I love your protectiveness, your hardworking nature, as well as your diligence and your humbleness. I hope to see you sooner rather than later." You can see that I didn't exclusively stick to my plan of complimenting the physical! For some reason I stopped at six! I failed my own physical compliment challenge!

My husband responded with this reply, "Thank you for those words, even though I don't deserve them or you. You are too kind. I love you. You made my day."

This must be why the Lord had the above question recorded in Scripture. It is a reminder for us to follow! We need to build up our men in every arena, including physical adoration. It will strengthen our love and our marital bed. Biblical principles always work, so compliment your man's handsomeness today! He is God's gift to you. He is the most attractive man you have ever laid eyes on!

MICHELLE KAUENHOFEN
Bothwell, Manitoba, Canada
reachaboverubies@gmail.com
Michelle is the Director of *Above Rubies* in Canada

BIBLE VERSE CALENDAR

I add little notes and pictures to my husband's lunch box. I try to write something specific that I love about him, or something encouraging to do with our life circumstances rather than general statements. I sometimes print off photos of us and our children and tuck them into his lunch kit. He loves showing off his family to everyone at work. Each night when I make his lunch for the next day, I grab a page off of our *Daily Bible Verse Calendar* and use the back side to write a note of encouragement. I used to write on plain note paper, but started to use the Daily Verse pages so that he could not only have encouragement from me, but from God's Word also.

REBECCA MCKAY
Prince George, British Columbia, Canada
bandb@ncol.com

I HEAR THE JOY!

I write my husband little love notes. I put them in his lunch bag or in his seven-day vitamin container. I write them on the outside of a banana. I write them on the mirror with lipstick. I'm sure I don't do it enough, but when I take the time to bless him in this way, I know it makes him feel special. He always tells me how much he appreciates the loving words, and I can hear the joy in his voice.

TINA SZYMONIAK
Rexford, Montana, USA
tinaszy@gmail.com

SWEET NOTHINGS

I leave sweet notes, sometimes praising him as a father, as a husband, or a wonderful and faithful provider. I especially like to leave little "sweet nothings" on slips paper for him to find.

DEBORAH GILCREASE
Tyler, Texas, USA
chefdebg@gmail.com

NO LONGER SEE HIS FAULTS

Sometime after we were married, it dawned upon me that this man I married was not all I had imagined. I started questioning what I was really doing being married to him. I could no longer see anything good—only the bad! These thoughts soon reflected in my behavior toward him.

Fortunately, I found an article that encouraged wives to look for ONE good thing in their husband and thank God for it. Not only did I do that, but I also thanked God for that quality when we prayed aloud together, e.g., "Thank you, God, for Chris and his patience with the children." This article also encouraged me to thank God for his manliness. I started thanking God in our prayers together for his strong muscles and the way he uses them to provide for us. Chris would thank me for my prayers and walk with a lighter step.

These prayers continued. My focus on one Christ-like quality grew and grew until I could no longer see the faults and thought more and more of my husband's fine qualities. In the process, Chris was greatly encouraged. Even today, the most encouraging thing I can do for him is to pray aloud for him and specifically thank God for his Christ-like qualities.

JANICE WILLS
Wairoa, East Coast, New Zealand

HEART-SHAPED LETTER

Last week I made a heart-shaped letter and wrote my husband a thank-you note. I thanked him for the little things he does, which most of the time I take for granted. I thanked him for putting the garbage out, for enlarging the dinner table when we have company, for cleaning the breadbox, and for giving me a cup of tea or a glass of water, etc. I slipped it in the daily pile of mail. I was upstairs when he got to read the mail, and it was so good to come downstairs and see him happily smiling. He put the little note in his pocket, and I noticed that later on he had it in his Bible.

WILMA SAMYN
Tongeren, Belgium
wilmam@skynet.be

BATHROOM MIRROR

One of my favorite ways to encourage my husband is to write notes to him on the bathroom mirror. He sees it first thing when he gets up. It lets him know I'm thinking about him in case we don't get to talk before he leaves for work.

SHELLY MONIZ
Brick, New Jersey, USA
Moniz8109@aol.com

NEW EVERY WEEK

When my husband was working out of town for a number of months, I decided to do something special for him every week while he was away.

The first week I hid love notes in his bags for him to find as he unpacked. The next week I hid encouraging notes and Bible Scriptures. Proverbs packs a wealth of great principles. The next week I wrote personal notes of things to talk to him about and sealed them with a loving kiss. I felt silly putting on lipstick that I never wear in order to kiss paper, but he appreciated it.

Another week the children and I wrote down all the things we appreciated about him. We marked them for him to open one each morning and each night. Yet another week, we wrote daily notes to let him know things we were doing on that day for him, such as cutting the grass, organizing his DVD's, or doing a small repair job on his "To Do" list.

CAROL VARGAS
Kennesaw, Georgia, USA
cjtazman@bellsouth.net

SECRET MESSAGE

It is my habit to leave little "love notes" for my husband to find. Sometimes it's just an "I love you" written on a steamy bathroom mirror so that when he showers the "secret" message appears.

SUSAN WHITEHEAD
Bailey, North Carolina, USA
affamily5@yahoo.com

LAST A LIFETIME

My husband is an auditory person who thrives on words of affirmation, and I've been getting better and better about learning to meet his needs! I write him lists of why I love him, explanations of how wonderful he is, or a story of how his assistance/being there has impacted me. I then plant them in strategic places! Some of my favorites are driving by his college and leaving one (plus some "sugar"!) in his car seat, stashing another in his duffel bag of work-out clothes, or on his pillow for him to find before he goes to sleep in the afternoon as he works midnight shift.

I am also working on becoming better at praising him. Even though I am not a verbal person, when I thank him and praise him for what he does, it improves our relationship. We're making our relationship one to last a lifetime, in accordance with the Word of God, and know that an ounce (or two!) of prevention is worth a pound of cure!!

HOLLY ANTHONY
Shawnee, Oklahoma, USA
blu_flye_737@sbcglobal.net

WELCOME HOME, DADDY!

I make a list of the qualities that I love about my husband to keep at my desk. Every month I mail Tom a romantic card to his work in which I expound on one of his qualities. It's a special treat for him to receive something personal at work. Tom really appreciates it, and doing this helps me to focus on his positive qualities and to maintain a heart of thankfulness.

Each Friday, the children and I make a sign for the front door which reads "Welcome Home, Daddy!" This helps make me more grateful as I focus on the fact that he commutes every day and has to leave us to support the family. After dinner each evening when Tom thanks me for the meal, I often say, "No, thank YOU!" because without his hard work we wouldn't have money for the food to make the meal.

NAOMI WOODS
Temecula, California, USA
naomiwoods1@yahoo.com

LUNCH BOX CONNECTION

Currently, my husband is working about a half hour away and takes his lunch with him. In each lunch box I sneak in a little note which sometimes becomes a long letter. I usually start with a Scripture at the top and then write my thoughts about it. He really responds to these. Once in a while, I write a letter full of the amorous thoughts I feel towards him. I try to remind him how thankful we are that he works so hard for our family. I've found I can be much more open and encouraging in writing. He often calls after he has eaten and read the letter. It gives us a real connection with one another throughout the day. He also saves all of them on his bed stand. When I miss putting a letter in his lunch box, he tells me how his day just wasn't the same. I spend anywhere from 5 to

20 minutes to write a letter. It's amazing what can come out if you just sit down with a piece of paper, a pen, and the Bible. Try it.

RACHEL HARRIS
Willamina, Oregon, USA
racheleigharris@aol.com

MAKE HIM SMILE

Once a month or so, I pull out some pretty paper and write to my husband. If I don't have pretty paper, I draw hearts and flowers on blank paper. Sometimes I glue pictures of us together to the front of construction paper. I express how much I love and appreciate him. This way he knows that the "little" things he does don't go unnoticed. I often talk about our dreams for the future, which spurs him on to *"fight the good fight."* I put my love letter in his lunch box, on the seat of his work car, under his pillow, or by the bathroom sink for him to find in the morning. I know my husband enjoys these love letters because for several days after receiving one, he has a huge smile on his face and holds his head up a little higher!

RASHEA COX
Hydesville, California, USA
Thecoxcrew@wmconnect.com

PROUD TO BE HIS WIFE

When my husband's had a rough day or going to have a rough day at a work. I sneak out in the middle of the night and leave him a note of encouragement, either in his wallet, on his cell phone, or somewhere in his truck. I may write something like, "I know times are tough, but we all appreciate your dedication and commitment to this family." Or "I am so proud of you. Our sons will only grow stronger having you as a father. You show them what a man, husband, and father is supposed to be, and I am proud to be your wife."

MISTY MARSHALL
Harris, Minnesota, USA
lamasahm@aol.com

PICK-ME-UP BINDER

For my husband, Jeremy's 33rd birthday, I asked family and close friends to send their words of encouragement to me via email—a favorite memory, a letter, a poem, a verse of Scripture, or a word of encouragement from the Lord. I then compiled these messages into a binder that Jeremy can read when he needs a pick-me-up.

LORIE DILLER
Boerene, Texas, USA
florenceflow@hotmail.com

KEEPING CONNECTED

My husband, a real estate broker, is very busy at work, and we often don't get to talk during the day. Some days I am aware that he is particularly stressed, and I like to send him email encouragement. I do this in the form of Scripture verses or a special moment we have shared in the past. He refers back to them during his hectic days. It keeps us connected and encourages him when he needs it!

NANCY PALMER
Newberry, Florida, USA
momto5@bellsouth.net

BEDSIDE THANKFULNESS

I have recently written a very long list of things I adore about my husband. I plan to print them out and leave a new one on his bedside table every night for him to read in the morning.

ANGELA STEWART
Harrison, Idaho, USA
tcstewart@gmail.com

MORE FREQUENTLY

I buy small blank white cards (about the size of a business card) from the News Agency, plus red and gold heart stickers. I stick one heart sticker in the corner of a card and write a brief love note or word of encouragement to my husband and put it somewhere for him to find it. Because the cards are small I can only write a few lines. That may seem a negative, but it means it is not as daunting a task as filling a whole sheet of notepaper and therefore I tend to do it more frequently. Because I use the same stationery all the time, as soon as my husband sees a card, he knows what it is and feels loved even before he reads it.

SAMANTHA BRYAN
Toowoomba, Queensland, Australia
Samantha.bryan@studentlife.org.au

HE WON'T FORGET

Once when my husband was going away on a business trip for a couple of days, I stashed little love notes everywhere for him to find, starting in his breakfast bowl, his shoes, under his keys, then in his clothes and toiletries to find at different times during the trip! He was reminded often what a great blessing he is to our family, and this, he says, encourages him to want to be an even better husband and father.

LIAN PEET
Belgrave Heights, Victoria, Australia
jpeet@ihug.com.au

T-SHIRTS

I special-ordered a T-shirt that says, "**I ♥ Doug**."

He is a fire-fighter, so another one I wear says, "**I'm in Love with a Firefighter**."

He gets a kick out of it.

DALYN WELLER
Yakima, Washington, USA
dailywalkinfarm@yahoo.com

Chapter 4

DRESS TO PLEASE

"You shall make holy garments for Aaron your brother, for GLORY AND FOR BEAUTY."
- Exodus 28:2

"Her clothing is fine linen and purple."
- Proverbs 31:22

"She dresses like royalty in gowns of finest cloth."
- Proverbs 31:22, NLT

"Awake, awake! Put on your strength, O Zion; put on your beautiful garments, O Jerusalem."
- Isaiah 52:1

DRESS MORE FEMININELY

Recently I have begun to honor my husband by dressing more femininely and lovely to look upon. I wear far more skirts than before. I wear bright colors and take care with my hair and make-up. My husband loves to come home and be greeted by a wife who has made a real effort to please him. He always says he loves me no matter what I look l like, but he is encouraged to know I love him enough to spend the extra time to delight him.

LOUISE SHAW
Geraldine, South Canterbury, New Zealand
shawtribe@paradise.net.nz

HE'S MORE IMPORTANT!

"How do I look honey?" I asked my husband. It was a Wednesday night and I was ready for the mid-week church meeting. I felt rather pretty with fresh make-up and clean clothes. My usual around-home appearance was disheveled and frumpy, so I knew I looked a lot better tonight. I was sure my husband would compliment me. Instead he said something I didn't like.

"Why is it that you dress up for others, but not me?" he asked.

"I cook, clean, and look after little children all day," I sputtered my silly excuses. Surely there was no reason to dress up for that. Couldn't he see that it was a foolish waste of time to make myself presentable unless I was going out? We had been married for eight years at that time and somewhere during those years I thought it okay to stop trying to impress my husband with my appearance around the house. Sure, I'd try to look nice if we ever went on a date, but that was a rare occasion. Making a regular effort to dress for your husband was for newlyweds, I thought.

I couldn't get his question out of my head that night as I tried to sleep. Why did I only dress up for others and not for him? When I allowed myself to admit the truth, it was very ugly. The reason was simply that I couldn't be bothered. It seemed such a waste of time to put on makeup or fix my hair when no one else but him would see me. I realized the unspoken message I was sending to my husband was a destructive one—he wasn't worth it.

I felt very silly when he arrived home from work the next night and I greeted him with a clean shirt, brushed hair, and make-up. "Have you been out?" he asked me, surprised by my appearance. Once he realized that my effort was just for him, he complimented me like he was courting me all over again. Just a few minutes extra on my part made him a happier man. Of course, it wasn't just the lipstick he liked. I was showing him that he was more important to me than anyone else.

It hasn't been a hard chore to set aside five to ten minutes to improve my appearance before my husband gets home from work. Since that time, I have made it a part of my routine. Some days are more chaotic than others and I can only snatch a couple of minutes, but there are days when I have a little extra time to make myself special for him. I love to see the appreciation in my husband's eyes.

Ask Your Husband

Not every husband desires his wife to wear make-up. Some men prefer their wives fresh-faced. Have you asked your husband how he likes you to look? Many women simply dress to please themselves or mimic the styles of the other women with whom they associate. Does your husband prefer you to wear dresses and skirts or does he love you in the sporty look of pants and jeans? I like to wear my hair up as my long hair drives me crazy while I'm working around the home. My husband loves it down, so before he comes home, I usually take it down and brush out the tangles.

Lose the Sweats

I have never met a person, either man or woman, who thinks baggy sweat pants and oversized T shirts are attractive. So often we gravitate to this sort of apparel because it is comfortable. This is also true with shapeless jumper dresses. (Ouch! Did I tread on some toes?) Let's face it; even the modest Amish women still have shape to their dresses—they do taper in at the waist. If you love wearing these sorts of clothes, but would also like to make more of an effort to honor your husband with your appearance, wear them during the day and then change before you greet your husband home. If you're blessed to have your husband working from home then you'll have to find some middle ground. Seek out comfortable clothes that still have feminine charm.

Dress with Purpose

Honoring your husband by dressing pleasantly for him is not a trivial matter! Queen Esther saved her whole nation because she presented herself in a beautiful and dignified way before her husband. The king offered her up to half of his kingdom, he was so pleased with her. Taking time for several minutes a day to honor your husband is not much compared to the full year Esther spent in beauty preparation. Esther 3:17 says she obtained grace and favor before the king. Verse 16 tells how he even proclaimed a holiday in her name. Do you think the king would have been so willing to grant her desire and save Esther's people if she appeared before him as so many of us appear before our husbands every night?

Dressing just for him also shows our children we respect and esteem our husband. My children are used to my daily transformation now. At first, they often asked if I were going out when they saw me come out of the bathroom looking much improved. I used these opportunities to tell them how much I loved their Daddy and how I wanted to look pretty for him.

The Two-Way Blessing

Not only is my husband blessed by my improved appearance, I am also. As I shed the day's soiled clothes and put on cleaner more attractive ones, I often feel as if I am shedding the day's frustrations. Whenever I've greeted my husband home looking awful, my mood has usually matched my appearance. It's easy to moan about the bad day you've had when you really look like you've had a bad day. When I feel better about my appearance, my attitude follows suit. Rather than just letting everything hang out and spewing negative nonsense from my mouth, I find myself smiling more and disciplining my tongue.

My husband is gone from 7.30 in the morning till 7.30 at night and sometimes later. I used to have a pity party over his long hours. Now I try to look at the good points. We usually save our special family meal for his night off, so on a general evening we can get our supper over with, clean up, calm down, and better focus on Daddy when he comes in the door. I find joy in this much better with my lipstick on. Instead of complaining, "You're finally home!" I'm ready to welcome my husband home with a smile and a hug.

PEARL BARRETT
Primm Springs, Tennessee, USA
pearlbarrett@yahoo.com

Chapter 5

THE WAY TO
A MAN'S HEART—FOOD!

WE CANNOT LIVE WITHOUT COOKS!

We may live without poetry, music and art;
We may live without conscience
And live without heart;
We may live without friends,
We may live without books;
But civilized man cannot live
without cooks.

He may live without books—
What is knowledge but grieving?
He may live without hope—
What is hope but deceiving?
He may live without love—
What is passion but pining?
But where is the man that can live
without dining?

- Owen Meredith

POUR OUT THE GRAVY!

I believe that one of the greatest ways we can serve our husband is to have a nourishing and aroma-tantalizing meal ready for him when he arrives home. This should be high on the job description for a wife, and yet it is not often seen as a priority today. I remember my husband's grandfather arriving to enjoy a meal with the family. As he walked past the kitchen window he would call out, "Pour out the gravy!" In other words, "I'm here! You can put the food on the table!" This attitude would be disdained my many today, and yet it was expected in grandfather's day that the dinner would be ready when the man walked in the door! Unfortunately, in scorning this delightful way of encouraging our husband, not only does the husband miss out, but the wife and family also.

If you postpone preparing the evening meal so that it is not ready when your husband arrives home, he is liable to go straight to the TV. A man feels like relaxing when he comes home from working hard, and many men use this as their relaxation. Unfortunately, it can then be difficult to get him to the table once he is seated comfortably in front of the TV. The secret is to have the meal ready when he comes in the door!

As you and your children greet your husband with excitement, you'll be able to say, "Honey, the meal is ready. You'll have time to freshen up while I put it on the table." Your husband can come straight to the table, drawn by the wonderful smells that waft from the food you have prepared. The lovely thing is that eating produces oxytocin, which is a calming hormone. Eating and fellowshipping together at the table relaxes your husband far more than sitting in front of the TV. Plus, you will enjoy the pleasure of his company.

Eating together at the table and especially enjoying family devotions together at the end of the meal will wash off the filth of the worldly atmosphere that your husband may have imbibed as he works in the secular world. Sitting in front of the TV will only add more filth of the world to his soul.

You will remember the beautiful story of how Jesus, who was used to the worship of angels in the glory of heaven, humbled himself to wash His disciple's feet. Peter was awed and replied, *"You shall never wash my feet!"* But Jesus answered him, *"If I do not wash you, you have no part with me."* Impetuous Peter then exclaimed,

"Lord, not my feet only, but also my hands and my head!" Jesus went on to explain to Peter, *"He who is bathed needs only to wash his feet, but is completely clean."* (John 13:1-11)

We do not need to be born again each new day, because the blood of Jesus has already washed away our sin and made our hearts clean. However, we do need to keep our feet washed, because it is our feet that get soiled and dirty in this filthy world. Your husband needs his feet washed at the end of each day. You do not need to literally wash his feet (although that may be something you are prompted to do on a special occasion), but drawing him to the table soon after he comes home, putting a nourishing meal in front of him, and filling him up with encouraging words as you share together will wash his feet like nothing else. The grime and the cares and the worries of the day will wash away. Your husband will be blessed, and you and your children will be blessed, too. It is worth your daily effort!

NANCY CAMPBELL

SUPPER'S READY

I have found that it means more to my husband than anything else I can do for him to come home to the aroma of a delicious dinner cooking—and also to find all of his work clothes ironed. These things show him that he is cared for and that I think of him during the day. This support encourages and uplifts him as he deals with all the stresses of the day.

KERENSA BLEVINS
Wake Forest, North Carolina, USA
blev7@mindspring.com

WHAT'S COOKING?

I encourage my husband by having dinner ready when he comes home. Even if it is not quite finished, to have something smelling good and nearly ready is a great blessing to him. I have noticed that he is so happy when he can sit and eat a fragrant, hot meal right away.

SANDRA GRAMMER
Aberdeen, Maryland, USA
bryangrammer9@msn.com

HIS FAVORITES!

My husband really enjoys certain foods, foods that often I don't think are nutritional, or that are boring to me. We have argued over food for 15 years! However, over the past year or two, I have felt he deserved more than I was giving him in the way of food. I began to think of what he would like for dinner, rather than what I think he should have. I now ask him what he would like before I make out the menu for the next week. I ask him what snacks he would like (he has hypoglycemia and needs to eat a snack before heading off to his graveyard shift where his job is physically hard on his body). I now prepare a breakfast he enjoys when he comes home from work in the morning,

I try to have foods that are special "daddy" foods on hand. I make the children respect him by not eating them all up before he gets to them. I teach them that their daddy works hard for us and that we need to have special treats just for him. I cannot please him every meal, but have found that when I make him happy through his stomach, he is happier all around. He looks forward to coming home to good meals that he enjoys. I now look for ways to encourage him instead of ways to make him holier and healthier!

Those ways weren't working. He was discouraged instead of encouraged.

JENNIFER PIERCE
Buhl, Idaho, USA
pierceroost@hotmail.com

SPOIL YOUR MAN

I was walking along the beach one day and the Lord popped into my heart to make my husband a sticky date pudding, as it is one of his favorites. Men love to be spoilt, especially when it comes to food! I believe that when you do something special for your husband, his heart will melt and soften. My husband loves the smell of home baking when he walks through the door. He still likes to lick the wooden spoon with the uncooked leftovers or lick the cream off the beater. He loves to have a cookie while it is hot out of the oven. Nothing beats home baking.

One of the best ways to keep a marriage fresh is to keep the romance alive. Communicate your love by expressing it in a practical way as well as verbal. Husbands are vision people. When they see the romantic scenes you create in your bedroom, bathroom, or at your dining table they get excited. They literally see that you think they are special. I like to set nice dinner tables. It is amazing what you can find in your home and garden to use for a table setting.

On one of our anniversaries, I invited married couples of all ages, and some engaged couples, to our home for dinner and entertainment. I asked one of our son-in-laws to sing *You are so Beautiful to Me* as each couple held hands and looked into each other's eyes. I decorated an arch in our doorway of the lounge with fairy lights and each couple took a turn at standing under it and sharing how they met. This was such an amazing evening, and all the couples talked about it for weeks afterwards.

One time when my husband was away, he wrote, "It is comforting to come home after a hard day at work to your lovely meals and candlelight dinners. I appreciate you and all the little things you do for me. They brighten up my day. I see the fruit of the Spirit coming out of your life with all the ideas He gives you."

ROBYN JOHNSTON
Gold Cost, Queensland, Australia
narj@savtek.net

Chapter 6

A LISTENING EAR

"Be more ready to hear, than to give the sacrifice of fools."
                                    - Ecclesiastes 5:1

"Bow down thine ear, and hear the words of the wise."
                                    - Proverbs 22:17

"The first duty of love is to listen."
                                    - Paul Tillich

*"It's just as important to listen to someone with your eyes as it is
with your ears."*
                                    - Martin Buxbaum

"Listen or your tongue will keep you deaf."
                                    - American Indian Proverb

LISTENING POWER

I encourage my husband by listening to him. I only offer my
opinion or advice when asked for it. I also always let him know
that I am praying for him and ask him specifically for things that
are on his heart.

JESSICA STRAWSER
Laurel, Maryland, USA
jessicastrawser@hotmail.com

LISTEN WITHOUT ADVICE

This is what I have learned to do to bless my husband.

1. Listen to him without any comments or advice.
2. Give him a five minute shoulder rub when he does not expect it.
3. Smile at him—a lot!
4. Ask him how his day was without including anything about my own day.

LORI CHIRICO
Lithia, Florida, USA
Believelc@aol.com

ASK QUESTIONS

I have found that simply LISTENING to my husband helps him a great deal. I ask him intelligent questions about his job and co-workers (and follow-up questions later), empathize with a problem he's encountering with a client, and take real interest in his world-away-from-home. By talking through these things with him, he often comes up with ideas, puts things in perspective, or just feels better about it.

JOAN JEWETT
Commerce Township, Michigan, USA
jjjewett@att.net

KEEP MY MOUTH SHUT

For as long as I've known my husband, he has battled low self-esteem. The greatest way I encourage him is to keep my mouth shut at "critical" times. It's so easy to say, "I told you so! You should have listened to me!" when he makes a mistake, big or small. I still have bouts of opening my mouth and then biting my tongue before saying too much. It's a constant, daily battle to keep the doors of my mouth under tight surveillance.

I try to give my opinion only when my husband asks for it. When he doesn't, it is hard to watch my husband make mistakes, especially with our finances. However, I enjoy seeing the Lord work in my husband's heart, something that I can only influence but not change. I know God wants what is best for His children, just as I do for mine. I want my husband to feel the freedom to lead. It is exciting to watch him grow in faith and spiritual understanding. Even though I am scared to death of the unknown territory we've begun to climb, my spirit feels victorious because I'm holding to God's unchanging hand.

ANGELA PRINE
Petal, Mississippi, USA
tchrmom22@yahoo.com

A QUIET WAY

I try to encourage my husband in a "quiet way." I do not nag him or interrogate him. I encourage him by loving him, being attentive to him, and doing my part as a wife and mother so that he does not have the burden to pick up my slack.

MELISSA ALLEMAN
Thibodaux, Louisiana, USA
ralleman@allemancpa.com

- Chapter 7 -

IT'S YOUR TOUCH!

DOMESTIC HAPPINESS

If a happy marriage has given and ensures to man peace at home, let there be no dread of the caprices of chance. A wife, gentle and affectionate, sensible and virtuous, will fill his whole heart, and leave no room for sadness. What will he care for the loss of property when he possesses this treasure? Is not his house sufficiently magnificent as long as she commands respect to it—splendid enough, as long as her presence adorns it? A cottage where virtue dwells, is far superior to a palace; it becomes a temple.

If he were deprived of a high and valuable office, he would scarcely notice it, for he occupies the first and best place in the heart of her he loves. Through her exertions, order reigns in his household, as well as peace to the soul. If injustice or ingratitude irritate or grieve him, her caresses will appease, and her smiles console him. Her commendation is glory; she, too, is his conscience; he thinks himself good when he raises her affections, and great when she admires him. He sees in her reason personified, and wisdom in action, for she feels all that the philosophers of every age have only thought.

Labors, pains, pleasures, opinions, sentiments and thought are in common between them; and, as she never expresses more or less than what she feels, he reads at a glance her thoughts, in her gestures; and, even in her eyes, he can apply to her what used to be said of Pompey when young: "The thought was uttered before the voice had sounded."

How easy and short does the voyage of life appear with such a companion! As in the Fortunate isles, he always finds in the same time buds, flowers, and fruits! His summer has retained and preserved the charms of his spring; and old age has drawn near without his perceiving its approach.

- Author unknown

HEAD MASSAGE

When I slip my hand behind my husband's head, he is instantly relaxed and calmed. A gentle rub of the scalp does wonders for his mood! Sometimes we are talking or he is reading the newspaper and I'll just start to rub the back of his head and all is well with the world. The best times are when my *Above Rubies* magazine arrives, and I read articles to him while massaging. He loves it and so do I!

HOLLY McLANE
Powell Butte, Oregon USA
mclanefarm@msn.com

AFTER EVERY MEAL

Quality time with one another is a must and has a positive effect on the children as well. When Dad and Mom are passionately in love, the children thrive. My husband and I always make a practice of hugging and kissing after we have a meal together, before he leaves, and when he comes home from work. The children don't miss much. When they see us hugging, they come running to do the same.

We also love our chat time before bed. It's a great time to unwind, share the details of our day--and a kiss and a hug always seals it. Our marriage is a daily commitment, not a once and done thing! When I put my husband and his desires first, I am always rewarded with a positive response back.

JEWEL NOLT
Lititz, Pennsylvania, USA
jewinbunch@dejazzd.com

A GREAT BIG KISS

Our van needed a new battery. My husband, Larry, checked on the price. Over $100 installed! He looked at me and said, "I can find it cheaper."

He did. But, installing a battery on our van is rather labor intensive and involves removing much of the housing around the battery. Gathering courage Larry said, "I'm going to go out there and rip it apart myself!"

I cheered him on as he left with all three boys in tow. Pretty soon our oldest stuck his head in the door and declared, "Mom, Dad says that he almost has all the necessary parts removed."

I replied, "You tell your Dad that if he succeeds, then he'll get a GREAT BIG KISS from me!"

Well, that just set them off! They came back a few minutes later and beamed as they reported, "He's putting the new battery in place!"

I said, "You'd better tell him to start puckering up. I'm sucking on a lemon to be sure I have a REALLY big pucker ready for him." They giggled and gave him my message.

Soon they reported, "Mom, the new battery is installed and everything is back in place!"

As they looked at me expectantly, I said, "Tell Daddy that he has to test it out before claiming his reward".

They raced outside with me close at their heels. Soon the engine roared to life and three boys yelled, "He did it!" Then six eyes watched (and who knows how many neighbors) as I grabbed their dad and laid a huge congratulatory kiss on him. The children applauded! This was also an encouragement to our children to see me take the time to thank their father for a job well done. And, of course, it was a lot of fun, too!

HOPE WARE
Peoria, Illinois, USA
lware@mtco.com

CHECKING OUR "LOVE TANKS"

My husband and I support each other by being honest with one another and talking regularly about how our "love tanks" are doing and what we could be doing better to love one another. For example, I need quality time, just talking and being together, Markus needs words of affirmation and physical touch. He loves me to tell him that I love him and to praise him for the good things that he does, He loves hugs and for me to put my hands on his back or head to show him that I love him.

SHAYNE SCHAFER
Lethbridge, Alberta, Canada
sschafer@telus.net

I TOUCH HIM EVERY TIME I PASS!

My husband is legally blind, which affects every aspect of his life. I encourage him every day by trying to make his life easier such as by doing tasks that require reading. I have never been a "touchy, feely" kind of person, but I decided when Don and I married that I would kiss him every time he left or entered the house. I would touch him every time I walked past him. I would tell him I love him every single day.

I consciously make the decision to never snap at him when he is frustrated or say something sarcastic to him in response. He tells me often how much he appreciates the things I do for him to make his life better. The funny thing is, the more I do for him, the more I benefit. We are more in love now than when we married. I now have an understanding of how much Christ loves us because of my husband's love for me, and our children also reap the benefit!

DIANA NASH
New Caney, Texas, USA
dlnash61@yahoo.com

HE KNOWS BEST!

I asked my husband how I can best encourage him because I thought he would know best! He answered, "By loving on me, hugging on me, speaking nicely to me, making biscuits and corn bread for me and looking sexy for me."

PELESIA KARSEN
Buncombe, Illinois, USA
pelesiak@hotmail.com

- Chapter 8 -

PHYSICAL INTIMACY

"Therefore shall a man leave his father and his mother, and shall cleave unto his wife, and they shall be one flesh."
- Genesis 2:24

"Derive delight from the wife of your youth; a lovely hind, a graceful doe, let her breasts satisfy you at all times, be always infatuated with her love."
- Proverbs 5:1-19 MLB

"You have made my heart beat faster, my sister, my bride; you have made my heart beat faster with a single glance of your eyes, with a single strand of your necklace. How beautiful is your love, my sister, my bride! How much better is your love than wine, and the fragrance of your oils than all kinds of spices!"
- Song of Songs 4:9-10, NASB.

"May my beloved come into his garden and eat its choice fruits!"
- Song of Songs 4:16, NASB

"The wife does not have authority over her own body, but the husband does; and likewise also the husband does not have authority over his own body, but the wife does. Stop depriving one another."
- 1 Corinthians 7:4-5, NASB

INCREASE HIS CONFIDENCE

The chances are good that your husband will not receive a great deal of encouragement in this dog-eat-dog world, so he especially needs to hear it from you. While verbal affirmation is vital, another often-ignored aspect is his need for physical intimacy.

Early in our marriage, I thought that everything had to be perfect in order for physical intimacy to occur. I thought the stars had to be in alignment, the candles had to be lit, I had to have the proper emotional input from him, and we had to have a good block of time.

Unfortunately, that scenario rarely happened, especially as children entered the scene? I found myself saying, "No" more often than I'd care to admit. Thankfully, the Lord began to deal with my heart. I remember reading a magazine article in which a wife took up the challenge to make love to her husband every night for a week. I was amazed! I decided to try it. I tried to arrange the perfection I thought was required, but after the second night, I learned that I could just participate without all the bells and whistles! I learned that quantity often leads to quality!

I've learned much since then. I've learned that all the times I said "No" were a blow to his self-esteem and were perceived as a rejection. I've learned that *my willingness to give of myself to him in this way is a huge encouragement to him and increases his confidence, as well as his marital satisfaction.* I've learned that the quickest way to give him a boost when he feels kicked around by the world is to initiate physical intimacy. I've also learned that if my husband is well-satisfied sexually, he will easily overlook a sink full of dirty dishes, or even do them himself!

TARA LAKES
Greenwood Indiana, USA
s-t-lakes@sbcglobal.net

SWEETER AS THE YEARS GO BY

I am a Filipino who served as a missionary in Papua New Guinea for eight years. That's where I met my husband, John, and we have now been married for over 19 years. I praise God for giving me a husband who loves, cherishes, and adores me! He counts me as his best friend, confidant, encourager, adviser, lover, and much, much more. He tells me that he is lost without me. But this has not always been the case. We had our challenges, trying moments, mighty mountains, rough valleys, and stormy seas along the way, but by the grace of God, we have victoriously overcome and have grown deeper in our appreciation, acceptance, and love for each other.

During our early years I would always go ahead of him! As a result, he felt I was overtaking his rightful place as head of the family. There were times when he thought I wanted to be the man of the house and was trying to make him my wife! This greatly affected his self-esteem. On those occasions, he withdrew from me instead of opening up to me. Whenever this happened, I felt the wall between us. I felt alone as I endured the consequences of my action.

I began to seek the Lord's guidance. Gradually, the Lord taught me how to submit to the authority of my husband, not just in word, but also in deed. Countless times, in obedience to God's command, I had to die to my own rights, opinions, feelings, and emotions (regardless of how right I felt they were) and yield to John's. I have found that this is the key to bring out the best in my husband.

One of the greatest struggles was in our sex life. Coming from a very conservative background where the topic was never discussed in our family, I had a lot of pre-conceived ideas, reservations, and wrong beliefs about the subject. As a result, I was not free to give myself fully to my husband. I gave lots of excuses and conditions before I gave myself away (especially with children coming every two years). This was very frustrating to him. *I discovered and learned the hard way that whenever I did not minister to him effectively in this area, it affected every other aspect of his being.* He would be grumpy and impatient about almost anything. On the other hand, when I fully ministered to him, I saw him at his best in everything.

I understand now that sex is a real need for a man and that this is the way God designed him to be. Regardless of how I feel, I must make every effort to meet this need, because no one else will (without him falling into adultery). It was a difficult process, but by the grace of God, I have learned my lesson. As a result, my husband is now happy, and I am enjoying the blessings of obedience to God's Word!

The amazing thing is that as I was going through the difficult and humbling process of learning how to submit to my husband, God was actually fighting the battle for me. On many occasions, after a storm has passed, my husband would realize how wrong he was and would come and ask for my forgiveness. As a result, he loved and trusted me more each time! Now, our love has indeed become "sweeter as the years go by."

Whenever John and I have differences, *I remember that my real enemy is not my husband, but Satan, who comes to "steal, kill and destroy."* (John 10:10) I determine to obey God's Word, regardless of how hurt I feel, because I want to defeat my real enemy. The amazing thing is that as soon as I yield to God's Word, I actually feel a sense of release and begin to see things from a different perspective—God's perspective. Every day I have to make a deliberate choice, whether to submit to my husband and reap the blessings of a glorious marriage or to rebel against his authority and suffer the consequences. Needless to say, I choose to do the former rather than the latter. When we submit to our husbands, we actually surrender to the Lordship of Jesus and as a result the blessings are endless. In the same way, when we rebel against their authority, we suffer the consequences of a troubled, chaotic marriage.

Now I know that it is possible to have a glorious marriage here on earth. Before I married John, my pastor's wife gave me one simple yet very profound advice: "*When everything (or everyone) around you becomes unlovable, DECIDE to love.*" I have taken this to heart, and I can say that it really works!

ARLENE LAVAKI
Sachse, Texas, USA
lavaki2003@yahoo.com

A HEALING BALM

One of the biggest ways I encourage my husband is to make love to him. When we lost our second baby in a year, the most important thing I could do for him was to lovingly initiate intimacy together. This also helped him to be able to open up to talk afterwards as we lay in each other's arms. As I was mourning, sex was not something I desired, but I gave myself wholeheartedly to my husband and it became healing for me too.

BECKY McKAY
Prince George, British Columbia, Canada
bandb@ncol.com

THE BEST TONIC

My husband needs encouragement the most when things get tough in the market place. During these tough times, I try not to get discouraged or to make demands of him that he isn't capable of delivering. Instead, I remind him of God's plan for him, pray with him, and greet him each day with a thankful, positive attitude.

Most of all, I make sure I fulfill all his physical needs with joy and passion. This is my husband's best tonic during challenging times!

LINNIE LUES
Durbanville, South Africa
Linnie is the *Above Rubies* Director in South Africa
linnie@aboverubies.co.za

Chapter 9

THE HATED WORD—SUBMIT!

"Wives, be submissive to your own husbands so that even if any of them are disobedient to the word, they may be won without a word by the behavior of their wives, as they observe your chaste and respectful behavior. Your adornment must not be merely external—braiding the hair, and wearing gold jewelry, or putting on dresses; but let it be the hidden person of the heart, with the imperishable quality of a gentle and quiet spirit, which is precious in the sight of God. For in this way in former times the holy women also, who hoped it God, used to adorn themselves, being submissive to their own husbands, just as Sarah obeyed Abraham, calling him lord."

- 1 Peter 3:1-6, NASB

"Marriage should be a duet—when one sings, the other claps."
- Joe Murray

WHY NOT SUBMIT?

I have to confess, I'm rather nosy by nature. I peer over my husband's shoulder whenever I notice him corresponding by e-mail. Thankfully, Charlie doesn't seem to mind my snooping, and I acquire some great information this way as he's not a real chatty person. Several weeks ago I read something in one of his e-mails that I found very encouraging. He wrote, "I am so thankful that I have a godly wife who is submissive to me." I hope repeating this won't make you think I'm trying to boast. There will be a point to this soon. Recently, while having dinner at my parent's house, Charlie praised me again by announcing the same thing to my family. And again, I overheard him making a similar comment to our pastor. The point is: *My husband values my submissive attitude above everything else I do. It blesses his socks off!*

Much has been written about submission, and it's common to hear many women speak of their struggles with it. I would like to share a different angle with you. I can't understand why any wife wouldn't want to submit. This may sound selfish, but there's a huge payoff. In Ephesians 5, it states clearly that the husband is the head of the wife. Is this to make her miserable, to tie her down, or to deny her getting her own way? No! God designed and created man to have this authority. Therefore, when we obey our husbands we allow them to fulfill this part of their lives. We complete them. It's a perfect fit. Not only are our husbands blessed, but they are then whole enough as men to turn around and cherish us.

His touch is tender when he realizes I won't dispute his leadership.

It's not hard for me to submit to my husband. I love watching his reaction when I affirm him and comply with his decisions. There's a softness that comes to his countenance when he realizes I won't dispute his leadership. His touch is tender.

The gift of submission is ours to give to our husbands. They cannot force it out of us. We may as well not call it "submission" if we do it grudgingly. The "Okay; have it your way!" attitude is not what this is about. *Webster's Dictionary* uses the words "'meekness" and "consideration" to describe this word. There is so much truth in the verse, *"It is more blessed to give than to receive."* Think about a special gift you have given to someone at Christmas time. Maybe it was a handmade gift that you spent time preparing and the person's response was so joyful and grateful that you felt blessed to be the one to bring such happiness. So it is with this gift of submission—there is a double blessing. When we submit willingly, we also harvest blessings for ourselves.

I don't know one woman who doesn't want a healthy, loving marriage, yet I've known many women who are not willing to surrender this part of their lives. Unknowingly, many women make marriage difficult for themselves. They take authority away from their husbands and wield it themselves, but sadly, it backfires on them.

A marriage does not work with two Adams.

Adam and Eve were not given the same job to do or the same role to serve. Adam was told to work and guard the Garden of Eden while Eve was made to be his helpmeet. Adam and Eve were each made to reveal different aspects of our Maker. Together, they make a complete whole. God knew how to create harmony with this order. A marriage does not work with two Adams. God has outlined a harmonious plan for our marriages in His Word. It's sad how many women have been taught an opposing doctrine by society—sometimes by their churches, and often by their own mothers.

My husband esteems me more because I choose to submit to him.

Submission is not repression. My heart goes out to the millions of Arab women who are not even allowed to show their faces because of the oppression they have been placed under by their religion. The Bible assures us in Galatians 3 that there is no distinction between male and female regarding our inheritance in Christ Jesus. There is no need to fear that submitting to your husband will cause you to lose your worth or to become a doormat. The opposite is true. My husband esteems me more, not less, because I choose to submit to him. He cherishes this gift I give him and has told me he is careful not to abuse it.

I can almost hear someone say, "But I don't have that sort of personality. I'm fiery and my husband is used to me being this way." God has made each of us to be unique, but don't let this be your excuse for not allowing your husband to lead your marriage. Although I am not this way myself, there are a couple of women in my family who are red-haired and have temperaments that match (perhaps you can guess who they are!) They are not "docile little women," but they know the value of submitting to their husbands, and they do it.

Okay, let's get practical. How do we submit? You don't have to wait until the next seriously important decision arises to allow your husband to lead. Submission is a lifestyle. I'll share with you some of the ways I have found to be effective. "I wanted to check with you first" or "Would it be okay if…" are phrases I often use with my husband. As mothers and wives we have households to run and many decisions to make daily. Of course, there are many things we must decide on our own, but this does not give us license to disregard our husband's leadership. The woman in Proverbs 31 whose price is above rubies brings honor to her husband. When making plans that will impact your family, check with your husband first before charging ahead. If he disagrees, this is not the time to rant and rave or give him the silent treatment.

My children know that daddy is in charge.

My children know that daddy is in charge. In my husband's presence I tell my children that Daddy answers to God for all of us. Believe it or not, it doesn't make me feel less of a person when my four-year-old goes around saying, "God's the boss of Daddy, and Daddy's the boss of Mommy."

Finally, when you have to make a decision on which you have strong feelings, you should feel free to share your thoughts with your husband on the subject. Remember though, as we are told in 1 Peter 3: 5, that a wife's meek and gentle spirit is precious in the sight of God. The way you share your feelings with your husband on the matter will affect his ability to listen. Remind him that you'll support him whether you agree with his final decision or not.

PEARL BARRETT
Primm Springs, Tennessee, USA
pearlbarrett@yahoo.com

IT'S FOR OUR BLESSING!

At fellowship time after church, a few couples were talking together about marriage. I asked the men, "What is the best way you like your wife to encourage you?" It was interesting that each husband replied, "I am blessed when she submits to me and allows me to be the head of the home." Gulp! I wonder why it is, that the very thing that blesses our husband the most is the one we try to avoid! Perhaps we'd better find out what God says about the subject?

1. Submission is Biblical

Many couples today believe they can get along doing things their own way, rather than standing on God's truth. But man's way doesn't work, as we see before our eyes with so many divorces taking place, even amongst God's people! Remind yourself of the Scriptures again: 1 Corinthians 7:3-4; 14:34b; Ephesians 5: 21-24; Philippians 2:6-10; Colossians 3:18; Titus 2:5; and 1 Peter 3:1-6.

The word "submission" is *hupotasso* and comes from two words— *hupo* which means "under" and *tasso* which means "to set in order." Therefore it means, "to place in an orderly fashion under something." Husbands cannot demand submission from their wives. We place ourselves under our husband's protection and leadership *"as unto the Lord."* It is something we do of our own accord, because we want to do God's will.

2. Submission is a heart attitude

Submission is not an outward act that we do under sufferance. It is a heart attitude. It is an attitude that is worked in us by the power of the Holy Spirit as we yield our will to the Lord. Most of us don't learn this lesson easily, but as we practice yielding, it becomes more a habit of our lives.

3. Submission is for our protection

God did not devise submission to bring wives into bondage. No, it is for our blessing, protection and covering. God's ultimate plan is for His female creation to be under protection throughout their entire lives—under their father's protection as a single person and then under their husband's protection when they marry. We see an understanding of this in the book of Numbers, chapter 30.

4. Submission is a kingdom principle

The word "submit" does not belong in Satan's kingdom. It is antipathy to everything that belongs to the kingdom of darkness. Satan's strategy is "independence." It was the spirit of independence and "I'll have it my way" that caused Satan to be cast out of heaven, and he continues to corrupt the world with this same spirit today. It may feel good at the time, but independence always ends in destruction. This is why we now have such an epidemic of divorce.

On the other hand, submission may not feel very natural, but it is a principle of the kingdom of God. The reason it doesn't feel natural to our flesh is because it is supernatural. It belongs to a kingdom of truth, light, and holiness. When we don't feel like submitting, it's because it goes against our fleshly nature. However, as we die to the flesh and yield to the power of the Holy Spirit, He will give us the grace to submit. As we flow in this kingdom principle, we will walk in the power of the kingdom of God. God's kingdom principles always work.

5. Submission is a picture of Christ and the church

Does the bride of Christ order him around and tell him what to do? Does she wear the pants? Is He not the head of the church? God planned for the marriage relationship to picture this truth to the world. Is our marriage a clear picture or distorted? Read Ephesians 1:20-23; Colossians 1:15-19; 2:9-10; and 1 Peter 3:22.

6. Submission wins the victory

Submission is not weakness; it is power. Submission is for the mature. It is a three-year-old mentality to stamp your feet and demand your own way. That's easy to do.

Jesus Himself gives the example. He sweat drops of blood as He anticipated His submission to His Father's will. He cried, "*Oh my Father, if it be possible, let this cup pass from Me: nevertheless not as I will, but as Thou wilt.*" In submitting to the Father's will, He won the greatest victory in the universe. He redeemed a people. He won a bride. He won the victory over death, hell, and Satan. When you are sweating it out, remember that you have not yet "*resisted unto blood.*" Read Matthew 26:39; Philippians 2:5-11; and Hebrews 12:2-4.

7. Submission takes faith

In 1 Peter chapter 3, we read the example of godly women who submitted to their husbands, even though their husbands were not believers, and even at times when they were wrong. But these women had a secret. They exercised the grace of submission toward their husbands, but they trusted in God! Even when they couldn't trust their husband's decision, they trusted God.

God is bigger than your husband! Remember that. When you think your husband is wrong and leading you down a wrong path, trust God. God will work for you as you put your trust in Him. Twice Sarah was taken into a harem, but she put her trust in the Lord, and God delivered her!

Be encouraged by these wonderful Scriptures with three powerful words. God delivered Sarah because she trusted Him!

Genesis 12:17 - *"And the Lord plagued Pharaoh and his house with great plagues **because of Sarai**, Abram's wife."*

Genesis 20:18 - *"For the Lord fast closed up all the wombs of the house of Abimelech **because of Sarah**."*

When you walk in a spirit of submission, you will receive seven blessings in your life. You will experience a…

1) Sensitivity to the work of the Holy Spirit in your life
2) Serenity—Soul rest and peace in your heart (Matthew 11:28-30)
3) Security and Stability
4) Sweetness
5) Soundness of doctrine
6) Strength of character
And you will be…
7) Saved from deception (Timothy 2:14-15)

NANCY CAMPBELL

Note: The above subject of Submission is only one of seven secrets to bring you into the fullness of all that God wants you to enjoy as a wife. To read the rest, go to www.aboverubies.org and go to *Articles and Stories.* Click on *Marriage* and then *Seven Secrets for Wives.*

PLEASE YOURSELF—YOU USUALLY DO!

The Bible was open before me and notes were everywhere as I waited on God to give me this anointed message on submission. You can imagine my shock when several hours into this study, God spoke to me and said, "Val, you cannot teach this message."

A little unnerved I asked, "Why not?"

His answer to my heart was, "Because you don't understand submission!"

Now I don't mind admitting that I was shocked. "Lord, do you realize that I'm Val Stares from *Above Rubies*? I've always encouraged submission."

"Yes," was the reply, "but you still don't *know* how to submit."

By now I was on the defensive. "But. Lord, you know that every time I want something, or desire to go somewhere, I always ask my husband first."

"And what is his reply?"

"He says for me to please myself. Oh yes, he always adds, 'You usually do.' I don't know why he says that, because he's already given me permission to do what I think best."

"If you are serious about learning submission, Val, I want you to go to your husband and tell him that from now on he needs to answer you, "Yes" or "No." If he says that you can please yourself, then you will take that as his disapproval and will stay home or go without. There is to be no pouting, no banging doors, no attitude of annoyance or hurt when this happens."

I desired to obey the Lord, so I bowled out to the shed where my husband could always be found and shared with him the plan that God had laid out before me.

"I can't wait!" he roared, laughing. "You'll never be able to do it."

I felt annoyed at him for thinking I was so weak, but it didn't matter, as I didn't want to go anywhere or have anything at that time. So far, the strategy was easy.

About three weeks later, a visiting speaker came to town. Everyone was excited. "Are you coming, Val?" I was asked. "Sure I will," I answered. "I wouldn't miss this for anything."

Finally it was time to ask my husband if I could go. Out to the shed I went, told him what was happening, and asked if I could go. As usual, I left everything until the last minute! Can you guess his reply? "Please yourself, you usually do."

Suddenly I remembered my pact with God. I was speechless as the enormity of the situation impacted my brain. I can't go! Worse still, I can't say anything. I raced into the bedroom and pleaded with God, "He's forgotten he has to say 'Yes' or 'No.' Can't I just remind him?"

"No" came the answer to my heart.

Perhaps pleading would help. "Lord, this is a special overseas visitor to our church. He may never come this way again. His message could change my life. I'm told I shouldn't miss his teaching."

"I'm teaching you," was the awesome reply.

By now you would think I would be still, but no, I had to have one more shot. "Lord, couldn't I just have a shower and get ready so that it will help to jog my husband's memory?"

"No!"

It was too much for me. I couldn't do anything. My emotions were getting the better of me. If I was going to obey God, I would have to divert them. I began cleaning the house to help relieve the tension.

Around the time I should have left for the meeting, my husband walked in to find me cleaning. "I thought you were going out to a meeting," he said.

You would have been proud of me. As sweetly as I could manage, and it wasn't easy, I answered. "No, Darling. Remember I told you that from now on I'm not going to please myself. God said you have to say 'Yes' or 'No,' otherwise I must stay home."

What do you think happened? He relented and said I could go? No. My husband is a gentleman and very slow to anger, but this time he was livid! "If you want to be so stupid, you can stay home!" he shouted as he stormed out.

It was then that the full revelation of what God was teaching me became clear. I had overridden my husband's decision so many times that he was now robbed of any desire to lead. He must have felt so cheated. Now, by God's hand, he was responsible for me staying home, but what hurt me most was the realization that it was me, the Christian wife, who had robbed him!

I wasn't bossy when we married. I just grew that way. My husband is a cautious man and rather slow at making decisions. My impatience at waiting for an answer caused me to make more and more decisions myself, and he would go along with me for the sake of peace. When you've got children hanging out for answers, it's easy to get caught up in this syndrome.

I stayed home for several weeks after that, while we both learned our respective roles. I thought I'd have to stay home forever! Gradually, my husband began to say "Yes" or "No" without the added adage of pleasing myself. As I continued to study the scriptures on the subject of submission, I realized that this was something I had to do of my own volition.

Ephesians 5:22 says, *"Wives, submit yourself unto your own husbands, as unto the Lord. For the husband is the head of the wife, even as Christ is the head of the church: and He is the savior of the body. Therefore as the church is subject unto Christ, so let the wives be to their own husbands in everything."* Are you like me and sometimes wish he hadn't written that last phrase?

Colossians 3:18 says, *"Wives, submit yourself unto your own husbands, as it is fit in the Lord."*

The Greek word for "submission: is *hupotasso* which means "to place yourself under." In each of the above Scriptures, God tells us "to place *ourselves* under our husband's authority." God is not telling husbands to make us obey or make us come under their authority. We do it because we love God and our husbands, and because He has asked us to. It is our choice.

In my mind I saw my broom raised to a horizontal position above my head. The handle was labeled, "My Husband's Authority." I could see that if he were in his rightful position, I would be able to walk beneath it in an upright position. This upright position was one of honor, security, love, and a surprise I didn't expect or notice until much later—power!

As I pondered my imaginary broom handle, I realized that I couldn't stand upright beneath my husband's authority. No, I would have to bend to get beneath it, mainly because he had been slowly robbed of his rightful authority, and secondly, because he now had no compulsion to take it up. My futile efforts only seemed to make matters worse. Just as my husband couldn't make me submit, I wasn't able to make him lead. Both were individual heart decisions. God gently showed me that I would have to learn to bend my attitudes until I could get under his authority. I had to become flexible. Just because the things I wanted to do were good things, didn't necessarily mean they were what my husband wanted to do. He could have other plans.

But then I realized that even bending wouldn't be enough to get under his authority. It would take more than a little bending. Perhaps, if I kneeled! Oh what a humbling position, but if that was what it would take, I would go that far. I realized that I was measuring myself against Bill instead of the Word of God. I was the one who was reading the Word each day, praying, and going to all the church meetings, and he wasn't. But God wanted me to measure myself by the attitude of Jesus.

We read about Jesus' example in 1 Peter 2:18-23: "*For what glory is it, if when ye be buffeted for your faults, ye shall take it patiently? But if, when ye do well, and suffer for it, ye take it patiently, this is acceptable with God. For even hereunto were ye called: because Christ also suffered for us, leaving us an example, that ye should follow his steps... who, when he was reviled, reviled not again; when he suffered, he threatened not; but committed himself to him that judges righteously.... Likewise* (with the same spirit of Jesus), *ye wives, be in subjection to your own husbands; that, if any obey not the Word, they also may without the word be won by the conversation* (the manner of life) *of the wives.*"

I had become so religious that I had failed to see that I would be pleasing the Lord more by obeying and submitting to my husband than by attending every church meeting and program.

However, it still wasn't low enough! There was only one position left! My husband's authority was so low that I had to lie down to get under it. Yes, I had to lay down my life! To get my marriage back into its rightful order, I took this position. I placed myself there. No one made me. It took sacrifice, and I had to lay down all my own rights. But I desired to be where God wanted me to be. It was the only position from where I could help my husband to take up his leadership role again. With God's help and guidance, I took one step at a time. The hardest part lasted only for a season. The rewards are for a lifetime and eternity.

What happened to that feared and dreaded "door mat," the so-called intimidated mousy wife who gets no say? It was a lie. It had no substance or power. I can now stand up straight, and walk upright, secure and loved under his protection. On this side of submission, I have more say because my opinion is of greater value than before.

One word of warning—submission is a daily practice, not a one-time act. I have to daily check my attitude and the humility of my heart.

VAL STARES
Beaudesert, Queensland, Australia
valstares@aboverubies.org.au
Val is the Director of *Above Rubies* in Australia

PUT HIM FIRST

I had been married for nine years when I finally stopped focusing on me and started putting my husband first. I used to jump all over my husband's case when I felt my needs were not being met. He felt so beaten down and "submitted" to me to keep the peace.

Now my husband is a confident and excellent leader, and I joyfully stand behind him. We have so much harmony and love in our home since I started this practice.

ERIKA SCHAMBACH
Elgin, Illinois, USA
Erika.schamlbach@sbcglobal.net

- Chapter 10 -

IT'S YOUR ATTITUDE
THAT COUNTS

Is there anything more beautiful than a home when the heavenly atmosphere is present? Atmosphere can make up for the lack of the luxury of wealth and the many comforts which money can buy, but the lack of atmosphere will rob of their charm possessions which are naturally beautiful in themselves.

A harsh word will chill the atmosphere of any home. A critical spirit, a manifestation of impatience, an unfair judgment, an unkind criticism, an undercurrent of restlessness, the absence of affectionate fellowship between husband and wife, the lack of accord between parents and children, the spirit of unfairness in one's dealings—these things all conspire to drive away an atmosphere, the presence of which makes a home like Heaven, but the absence of which makes beautiful living most difficult, if not quite impossible.

The lack of atmosphere may be detected at the threshold of the house one is about to enter, and when one has crossed this threshold, no amount of interior decoration, no lavish display of that which money can buy, no forced cheerfulness can take its place, or make up for its absence.

It is present in a home when kindly words are spoken; when the members of a household live in right relations with each other; when all speed is used to right a wrong or to ask forgiveness for the word which should not have been spoken or for the deed which should not have been done. Most of all, this atmosphere is ever found where He is present, Who being in such a home is the unseen guest and the silent listener to every conversation.

- Wilbur Chapman
When Home is Heaven

ENJOY!

One of the major ways to encourage my husband is to enjoy being his wife. I enjoy having him be the breadwinner while I stay home with his children. I enjoy teaching his children and being the keeper of his home. An attitude of thankfulness, respect, and love goes a long way to let him know he is appreciated.

MARTHA PERRY
Riverbank Kings CO, Nebraska, Canada
perryfamily@gmail.com

CAN YOU LET GO?

Is your husband "free to be" whatever that might be? What if he really is so selfish that if you let him be, he wouldn't help you with the dishes even one night a week? What if he really would watch television from the moment he walked in the door until it was time for bed? Or, in my case, what if he really would sit in front of the computer for 16 hours a day? What is that thing that your husband would do if left unchecked by you? What would your life look like if you never once checked anything your husband did—how he spent the money, how he spent his free time, if he went to church, or how he handled the children?

My next question is, do you trust the Lord? Do you trust the Lord enough to allow Him to deal with your husband? What if God never addresses those issues that we deem important? Would you still keep your fingers out of the pot?

As wives, we very often get in God's way when it comes to the heart of our husband. Allow me to give you an example: your dear husband walks in the door from a long day at work and is grumpy. Even after he has had his 30 minutes of uninterrupted unwind time, he is irritable. Your darling children are eager to have some attention from their daddy and converge on him as he comes back down to join the family. His response to them is harsh and, obviously hurt, the children slip away. How do you handle his situation? Do you call your husband to task for being harsh? When we do this, we put ourselves right in the middle. Our husband gets caught up in justifying himself to us instead of to God. Since this is never our place of authority, everyone loses. It is better to duck so that we are out of God's line of fire. Let God deal with your husband, directly.

Do you trust Him enough to meet the deficits? God picked you and your husband to be the parents of your children. When he did so, He took into account ALL of the deficits. Our position of authority in these situations is on our knees, asking God to pour out His grace on our hurt children and to draw our spouse closer to Himself. We need to repent for trying to be our husband's Holy Spirit. We need to repent for the real root, which is fear and unbelief. We haven't trusted God. We haven't believed that He is able to reach our husband's heart, so we've tried to do it for Him.

What happens when you stop parenting your husband? It's not the answer you would like—things may get worse. They get worse because all of a sudden your husband is free to be REAL. He may really be the kind of guy that, if left to his own devices, would spend every free moment in self-indulgence. This can also be attributed to the way we all respond when we are set free. We go HOG WILD.

There are ways you can actively walk this out in prayer. The first is to repent and give up your rights. We all have rights and our society has trained us to demand them. When we do, we are actively trying to control the people around us. In this case, it is our spouse. The second way is to praise and thank God. Praise Him for the lack in your life and thank Him that He has allowed it to make room in your life for Him.

I have been married over 17 years. As the Lord has helped me to walk this out in my home and marriage, I have learned that the root of fear and unbelief goes deep in my life. I have built safety nets all around me and have tried to control anything I get my hands on. I have actively had to repent and hit my knees to walk this out. I've had to do a lot of reprogramming. The most unexpected result is the LOVE that has grown in my heart for my husband. This is what unconditional love looks like. You choose to accept who your husband is and stop trying to change him. In turn, he begins to trust you, and you become a safe place for him.

Sometimes, this can bring out ugliness, because we can be our worst in our safest places. But in this REALNESS of who we are, no longer pretending or manipulating, God isn't held back by a fantasy that we have created. We need to lean into our pain and embrace our brokenness. God is able to work directly on the reality of who we are, who our husbands are, and what our families are. We are all broken, needy, and naked. When we try to deny this, we hinder God from healing, providing, and clothing. This real growth, God's growth will not burn up, but will come through the fire as purest gold.

Did my husband stop spending 16 hours a day on the computer? Yes and No. But the fighting between us has all but ceased. I learned that my disapproval of him pushed him away from me and the children, thus causing him to withdraw from the family and to spend more time on the computer. Our home is much more peaceful, and I am able to trust God for the needs that go unmet when my husband is on the computer for hours on end. My husband is very artistic and works with computer graphics, digital photography, and web design—all as a hobby. He is a drywall/steel framer by trade. I was unable to enjoy his gifting because I resented the time he spent on it. As the Lord has helped me to accept who He made my husband to be, I have become free to love and encourage him.

Let God be your protection and strong tower. The people in our lives will, and do, let us down. They hurt us and neglect us at times. If they didn't, we would have no need of Jesus. Our children will be hurt and disappointed. When it happens, if we are veterans at embracing our brokenness, we will be equipped to walk them through theirs.

PAMELIA STEPHENS
Shelton, Washington, USA
pameliasue@msn.com

A CAPTIVATING WIFE

I often ask myself, "Would I do this if we were courting?" This little question has gone a long way to build our marriage.

After the birth of my second baby, I was always busy. One afternoon, tired and frustrated, I snapped at my husband. He is not one to retaliate, but he picked up our new baby, and loud enough so I could hear, he said, "Your Mama used to be so sweet. What happened to that sweet woman I married?"

Shamefully, I realized he was right. He fell in love with the sweet me, the one who hung on his every word. He would tell me my voice was soothing to him and my smile brightened his world. Sure, I knew he had faults, but I chose to ignore them. He was the hero of my life.

I had allowed myself to come to a point where my voice was no longer soothing. Instead, it was nagging or whining. My smile, I am sorry to admit, wasn't showing as much. Now, instead of ignoring my husband's faults, I tried to fix him. I hadn't turned mean and nasty, but I wasn't the same doting bride.

I determined to change. My husband did not deserve a snappy wife. Being busy was no excuse. But have you noticed that simply trying hard to be better doesn't usually work? I was still tired most of the time from being up at night with the baby, and my work load often overshadowed my determination to be kinder toward my husband. I often felt under-appreciated and missed the compliments he used to give me.

Proverbs 5:18 says, *"May you rejoice in the wife of your youth."* The next verse says, *"May you ever be captivated by her love."* I earnestly wanted my husband to be captivated by me. I knew he had a strong love for me, but I wanted to be a wife that he could still rejoice in. I realized God wanted this for us, too. Years of familiarity did not have to take their toll. If God's desire was for a man to always stay captivated by his wife, then I knew He could help me be that sort of wife.

New understanding dawned in my heart. I had a big part to play if I was to be a doer of this Scripture, not just a hearer. Proverbs says it is a wife's love that keeps her husband captivated. A man doesn't stay captivated on his own. My husband would never have fallen in love with me if I had been down in the mouth while we were courting. How could I expect him to rejoice over me when this was how I was acting now?

If I wanted him to treat me like he was madly in love with me, I needed to offer him the sweetness and admiration I showed when our love was new. Even if he didn't react the way I hoped he would, I learned from these Scriptures that this was what God desired, and I needed to obey.

Instead of dismissing my husband's opinion and arguing with my own, I began to ask myself, "Is this what I would say if we were courting?" Sure, we might disagree on things, but I would never cut down his opinion in a haughty tone. Would I look disheveled and frumpy if we were courting? No way! I would dress to please him. Would I let my frustrations show during trying moments when we were courting? Rather, I would most likely cry on his shoulder and tell him I could never get through this situation without him.

This courting question has never failed to remind me that I do have a choice when it comes to my behavior. Sure, it is much easier to throw a fit than to stay even-tempered. It is easier to snap or give a cold shoulder than to respond kindly. I'm far from perfect, and I don't always choose the right reaction, but I have learned that giving in to unkindness hurts me just as much as it hurts my husband. I push him away with harsh reactions. A man is captivated by a woman who treats him like he is her Knight in Shining Armor. He wants to stay close to that sort of woman.

In recent years, I feel more cherished by my husband than ever before. Sure, all those fuzzy-wuzzy feelings of new love have settled down, but in their place something deep and far more beautiful has taken root. My husband, who rarely thought about giving me flowers in the early years, sometimes surprises me with roses. I feel so blessed when he tells me I'm the most perfect wife a man could have. I have to chuckle at this. I know for certain I'm not a perfect wife, but a captivated man is not interested in his woman's faults.

Imagine you and your husband were courting again. Wouldn't you respect him? Admire him? Appreciate him? Encourage him? Smile at him? Tell him how you love him? Laugh with him, not at him? Dress for him? Try to impress him with your cooking? Show him affection? Hang on his words?

Although none of us can hold on to our youth forever, we can still be the wife that our husbands rejoiced to receive on their wedding day. We can continue to be a captivating wife.

PEARL BARRETT
Primm Springs, Tennessee, USA
pearlbarrett@yahoo.com

FIND HIS LOVE LANGUAGE

I have found out that I need to know my husband's "love language." My love language is gifts, so when we were first married, I always bought my husband nice gifts for his birthday, Christmas, and Father's Day. I was so excited about it. He was gracious and appreciative, but never as excited as I was. Matt is much more excited when the children and I write him notes of love and appreciation and when I have a clean house and nice dinner ready for him. Now I know this is what he really wants and needs, I don't feel bad if I haven't gotten him a "purchased" gift. I have realized that his love language is words of affirmation (receiving gifts is probably his least important one). To this day, my husband encourages me verbally, which it is nice, but it isn't something that really touches my heart, so he occasionally sends me flowers or brings home a candle or other treat. Finally we've figured out what the other truly wants and needs to feel encouraged.

DANIELLE HULL
Columbia City, Indiana, USA
mdhull@kconline.com

DON'T LISTEN TO DESTRUCTIVE THOUGHTS!

Many years ago our marriage was hurting. Stuart was in University getting a Bachelor's of Education, our first son was almost three years old, and our precious baby was newborn. The pressures of becoming new parents, trying to discern how to live a Christian life that was pleasing to God, financial pressures, and the tension of hurts from our past were too much for me to handle. Stuart and I grew distant in our hearts toward one another. We built stone walls around our hearts. We argued and hurt one another with words.

I allowed my feelings to control my thought patterns, rather than subjecting them to the Lord. "This is not what I want for the rest of my life! I don't deserve this," I thought. The thoughts grew louder and played more frequently, "He is so ugly. How could I ever be attracted to him again?" Or "If he only knew the pain in my heart …but even if he did, he is so cold, it wouldn't affect him." It first happened during an argument. I yelled to Stuart, "Maybe I should just get this pain over and divorce you!" I suddenly realized the destructive power of these words, but my heart was hardened and I rationalized it away.

Later that afternoon, I phoned a dear friend of ours and told him what happened. He hung up without speaking and five minutes later he was knocking on my door. Gordon was a calm, shy and quiet man, but not today. He burst into my entranceway and in a loud voice said, "Don't you EVER allow such words to be in your mind or heart again! God HATES divorce! Divorce is a sin! As soon as you allow the first hint of a thought and do not take that thought in obedience to Jesus Christ, it will grow. The devil wants you to play with the idea until it becomes reality. He will then laugh because another Christian marriage has been destroyed! Immediately repent and turn away from such thoughts!" He turned around with tears in his eyes and left.

I sat stunned. Every word he spoke was true. Every word! I had allowed a sinful thought to grow and had fed it until it almost destroyed our home and children! I knelt down right where I was and cried out to God to forgive me. I cried out for my marriage, my husband, my children, and the horrible future they almost faced because of who I had become.

2 Corinthians 10 2:5 says, *"Casting down imaginations and every high thing that exalts itself against the knowledge of God, and bringing into captivity every thought to the obedience of Christ."*

I started to pray for our marriage. Every day I prayed, "Father, please forgive us both. Please tear down my walls, stone by stone, that I built up, separating myself from my husband. Oh God, give me a new love for him. I forgive him, but help me to feel this feeling of forgiveness deeply. Oh Lord, please help me to love my husband unconditionally as you love us. Place a shield of protection around our marriage so the fiery darts of the evil one cannot penetrate. Let our marriage blossom into a testimony that points directly to you, Oh Lord. Thank you for saving our marriage."

God heard my prayers and healed our marriage. It did not take long at all until God restored my love for Stuart. He knit us back together again into a beautiful God-honoring relationship.

ORLENA WEAVER
Ontario, Canada

ATTITUDE SETS THE TONE

After 30 years of marriage, I can tell when my husband is in need of special encouragement. When I feel that tap on the shoulder from the Holy Spirit (or am faced with an obvious need from a tired, discouraged husband), I try to assess the situation and figure out what the situations warrants. Probably the #1 way to encourage him is to make sure his physical needs are met by a nice hot meal and clean clothes and private husband-and-wife time.

Some extra attention like a backrub or cuddling on the couch helps, too.

Usually he takes care of the outside chores of our home, but to encourage him, the children and I will make sure the yard is extra neat and perhaps straighten up the garage. Homemade cards from the little ones and special prayers of thanksgiving for him during devotions are little ways to encourage him. Sometimes he just needs words of admiration and affirmation from me, including cheerful "permission" for him to be gone from the home for his duties as a pastor.

My attitude sets the tone of the home, and that is a big part of encouraging my husband.

CHARLOTTE SIEMS
Stillwater, Oklahoma, USA
fruitvine@aol.com

"The attitude of your heart will determine the atmosphere of your home which will in turn affect your marriage and ultimately the actions of each member of your family."

NANCY CAMPBELL

- Chapter 11 -

MAKE TIME FOR YOUR HUSBAND

TO MY DEAR AND LOVING HUSBAND

If ever two were one, then surely we.
If ever man were lov'd by wife, then thee.
If ever wife was happy in a man,
Compare with me, ye women, if you can.
I prize thy love more than whole Mines of gold,
Or all the riches that the East doth hold.
My love is such that Rivers cannot quench,
Nor ought but love from thee give recompense.
Thy love is such I can in no way repay;
The heavens reward thee manifold I pray.
Then while we live, in love let's so persevere,
That when we live no more, we may live ever.

- Anne Bradstreet

OUR CUP OF COFFEE

As wives, we often get so caught up in laundry, cooking, baking, cleaning, and being a mommy that we forget that we are wives also. Realizing this, John and I have established a tradition in our marriage. We both get up earlier than the children. No matter what time that is, the children are not to come out of their rooms until we have had a cup of coffee together. This is my treasured time to start my day with the one I love. The older children play with the smaller ones while Mommy and Daddy have their time together.

Not only does this give us a beautiful start to our day, but it also shows our children that we love and honor one another. I am raising future wives and husbands, and I want them to cherish their husbands and wives the way we do to one another.

LAUREL SIMPSON
Fort St. John, British Columbia, Canada
jlsimpson@net.kaster.ca

JUST BEING THERE

A few years ago my husband changed occupations from constructing pole barns to owning a small engine business. The first few weeks were difficult, especially learning how to do the bookwork. My husband spent many evenings at the store, and often the children I stayed with him. From the beginning I wanted to be involved, because I knew this was the best way for me to understand what he was facing, and if he had to work late, I could deal with it better. Kevin has told me many times how much it means to him to have me come into the store, even when I feel I'm not actually doing much. Just my presence is an encouragement to him. Of course, that encourages me to keep on encouraging him.

IRENE MILLER
Seymour, Missouri, USA
Kevinirene34@hotmail.com

WISE USE OF MY TIME

As a young mom, I thought of the time when my husband came home as "my time to get things done," because he was there to spend time with the children. One day my dear husband asked me why I didn't spend time with him anymore. What he meant was, "Why don't you sit with me like we did before we had children?" At first, I thought it would not be a wise use of my time, but soon realized otherwise.

Now when he is home, I try to be in close proximity to him. I was cleaning in my room the other day while he was putting a bookcase together. I remembered his statement and went and worked in the same room he was in. A few minutes went by, and he remarked how nice it was to be together. I didn't even think he knew I was there! It made him feel loved and encouraged him in a job that he really didn't relish.

VICKI SCULLY
Marlton, New Jersey, USA
happywithmyfive@comcast.net

CULTIVATE TOGETHERNESS

Do you know what the relationship is between your two eyes?

They blink together!
They move together!
They cry together!
They see things together!
And they sleep together!

I am always looking for ways to encourage my husband to like being *with* me. After all, that is one of the BIG reasons we married—so we could be together. Now that he is retired, instead of shooing him off to seek enjoyment somewhere else while I am busy, we work at how we can be together. We agree together before taking the next step. We shop together. We care for his 82-year-old sister together. We often cook together—especially when Bill makes his wonderful curries. Bill helps me with *Above Rubies*, collecting them from the wharf and then packaging and mailing.
Bill is very much a man's man and spends many hours in the shed fixing things for everyone. He also fixes the things I break! To be honest, I'm not as good at helping him as he is me! However, I often pop my head in the shed and encourage him in his work.

We are both aged pensioners and after all the years of fostering togetherness, I am now reaping the wonderful reward of loving having my husband around me 24/7!

VAL STARES
Beaudesert, Queensland, Australia
valstares@aboverubies.org.au
Val is the Director of *Above Rubies* in Australia

HE NEEDS ME

I encourage my husband by spending time with him every evening before he goes to work. This is not always easy to do because I would much rather be curled up with a good book after the children are in bed than on the couch watching movies. But I have found that he needs me spend time with him (yes, even in front of the TV).

We also like to play scrabble or other board games together. Other times my husband needs me to relax with him and not even talk, something that is very hard for me not to do. During these nights he studies the Bible, history or science books and tells me what he has learned from them. During these nights I curl up with my book on the couch and put it down when he has some interesting tidbit to contribute to the silence.

I am no way near perfect but God has shown both of us that by putting ourselves last we have more peace and joy in our home. The children are seeing two parents who love each other and are trying to please each other.

JENNIFER PIERCE
Buhl, Idaho, USA
pierceroost@hotmail.com

Chapter 12

DON'T FORGET TO PRAY!

"God forbid that I should sin against the Lord in ceasing to pray for you."

                                        - 1 Samuel 12:23

TO MY HUSBAND

I said a prayer for you today.
I just took a moment to say,
With heartfelt thankfulness,
How much I know I'm blessed
With the love so deep and true
That I receive from you.
It may not always show,
But darling, I always know
That God gave you to me
And I will ever be
A grateful, loving wife
All throughout my life.
I love you with all my heart
And we will never part.
I know this love will last.
And so a day will never pass
In which I cannot say:
I said a prayer for you today.

                        - M. Heale

PRAYING PROVERBS

Something I started doing the month before Todd and I married was to pray through the day's Proverbs for him (i.e. Proverbs chapter 1 on the first of the month). I've continued this practice and have started to include the Psalms as well. I rotate through all of them. Since he does construction and I usually pack his lunch, I write him notes and include verses from the chapter in Psalms or Proverbs that I prayed through most recently (i.e. the note I write one day usually ends up in the next day's lunch). I write the date and verse on one side of an index card and a note on the other side. I start the note by thanking him for something relating to the verse and him and then mention what else I'm praying for him.

PAULA SMITH
Pleasantville, TN, USA
revelation21_45@yahoo.com

PRAY SPECIFICS

Tom and I had been married four years when I went to a meeting at a local church. I was disappointed when I arrived that the person I wanted to hear was not speaking. Instead, it was his wife who shared that she had not been praying for her husband the way she should. It was an eye opener to me. I realized I was guilty, too.

When I got home, I told Tom about my lack of prayer for him and asked his forgiveness. I realized I did not know how to pray for my husband. I asked the Lord to teach me. The Holy Spirit immediately showed me to go to my concordance in the back of my Bible and look up the word "integrity". I wrote all the integrity verses on a legal pad ready to pray them. I could hardly wait for Tom to leave for work. As soon as he left, I would pick up my legal pad and start praying for him. Here's an example from Psalm 25:21, "Lord, may integrity and uprightness protect Tom, because his hope is in you." I prayed the integrity Scriptures for one week. After that, the Lord directed me to a different topic to pray for my husband. As long as I am open to the Lord's leading and guidance, He continues to show me how to pray for my husband.

PATRICIA FOBES
Colorado Springs, Colorado, USA
prayergirl55@yahoo.com

NOTHING BETTER THAN PRAYER

I believe the greatest way we can encourage our husband is through our prayers. Here are some questions I ask myself. I found these at http://www.doorposts.com/Samples/aul_prayer.pdf , but have added my own comments.

Do I earnestly pray for my husband's spiritual growth and wisdom as he leads our family?

I pray that my husband seeks to know God and His plans for his life. I pray Paul's prayer in Colossians.1:9-12 for him. I pray earnestly for my husband as he leads our family. I pray that he will actively seek God in all that he does. I pray for the Lord's wisdom as he answers our children's questions about spiritual matters.

Do I pray for my husband in his work, his leadership responsibilities, and his relationships with others?

As my husband interacts with the people he contacts at work, I pray that he will lead a godly and honest life, one that reflects the saving grace of the Lord Jesus Christ. I pray that those around him might see the difference that God has made in his life. How often we forget that our husband's mission field is his workplace.

Do I pray for a reverent heart and submissive response to my husband?

I have learned that neglecting my spiritual walk to do other seemingly important tasks benefits no one, especially me. I serve the Lord through serving my husband. I am learning God's will as I show reverence to my husband. I cannot be the wife that God has created me to be if my heart is not right with Him.

Do I pray for my husband's relationship with each of our children?

In Malachi 4:6 it says that a father's heart is to be turned towards his children. I pray daily that my husband's heart is turned toward his children. I pray that he will see the individual needs of each child and that God will guide him as he interacts with them.

Do I pray for my husband when I know he is going through times of testing and hardship?

We are to *"bear one another's burdens."* (Galatians. 6:2) We need to be mindful of what our husbands are going through. I make it a point to find out what is bothering my husband so I can pray specifically. I will ask him, "How can I pray for you today?"

Do I pray for my husband to be strong in his particular areas of weakness and temptation?

I know that many temptations face my husband daily. I usually try to pray a prayer of protection over him as he walks out the door each morning. It is getting harder for a man to stand strong in this world when everything relates to a humanistic value system with no fear of the Lord. But God will deliver the godly out of temptation (2 Peter. 2:9).

When my husband is in sin or when I believe he is making an unwise decision, do I humbly entreat him and then earnestly, patiently, and quietly pray for God to lead him?

I sometimes lash out at my husband if he is wrong or makes a bad decision. How many times have I said something only to regret it two seconds later? Why don't I remember God's word in Exodus 14:14, *"The Lord will fight for you, and you shall hold your peace."* I know that my husband's heart is in God's hand and He will turn it as He wills (Proverbs 21:1). I try not to say, "I told you so" when God does change his heart, but instead give the glory to the Lord, for He deserves the praise.

Do I pray for my husband when he has offended me, or do I criticize and harbor bitterness?

I pray that God will hold my tongue in situations like this. In Proverbs 21:9 and 19 it says that it is better to be anywhere else than with a brawling, angry women. I am a miserable woman to live with when I have been (or think I have been) wronged. It is important to be open with your husband about your feelings. I am usually surprised my husband didn't even know he had hurt me. I pray for the Lord to help me forgive, move on, and forget. What if God kept on recalling our past sins all of the time? Let us not do this to our beloved husbands.

HEIDI KEMP
Nassau, Bahamas
the_kemps_nas@yahoo.com

NO RECORD OF WRONGS

I remind my husband that the battle is not against flesh and blood, and therefore I am not his enemy. When things get tense, we talk it out together before we have a blowup or build up a wall between us. We pray together every night and make sure we do not keep a record of wrongs.

SANDI ZAGEL
Fishers, Indiana, USA
Sandi.Zagel@uscm.org

Chapter 13

JUST DO IT!

SAY THEM NOW!

If you have kind words to say,
SAY THEM NOW!
Tomorrow may not come your way,
To do a kindness while you may,
Loved ones will not always stay,
SAY THEM NOW!

If you have a smile to show,
SHOW IT NOW!
Make hearts happy, roses grow,
Let the friends around you know
The love you have before they go—
SHOW IT NOW!

ANYTHING TO HELP

I like to do whatever I can to help my husband. Each morning I love to prepare my husband's breakfast, warm his towel while he showers, start his car, take anything he needs for work to his car for him, and clear his car of snow, if needed.

Occasionally, I send a card or letter to him at work, thanking him for working hard so that I can stay home with our children. We email back and forth throughout the day and talk on the phone. Our conversations during works hours last only a minute, but I can get a feel for how his mood may be upon arriving home. If I think he may have had a stressful day, I have a salt bath drawn for him to soak in when he gets home. I also keep a prayer diary of requests from him and for him and remind him that I am praying for him.

The best complement I have ever received came when he said I was a better wife than he ever thought any wife could be. Our marriage has been blessed by a willingness to do whatever needs to be done for each other.

SARAH COPE
Bloomington, Illinois, USA
saraithehuntress@hotmail.com

TRY SOMETHING NEW!

One night on a date with my husband, I opted to do something that I knew would bless and encourage him! Attend a *free* fishing seminar together. Gulp! I wasn't overly thrilled about it at first, but supporting his interest truly spoke volumes to him. He hasn't stopped talking about it to his buddies either. We are now ocean fishing together, and I am really enjoying it! I'm even learning the fishing "terminology!"

SANDY SCHMIDT

TAKE ACTION!

I have found that the best way to encourage my husband is to take action! It's not enough to think about it. Here is an acrostic about ENCOURAGE that has helped me to take action.

E = Eye Contact

Shoot encouraging glances toward your sweetie. Let him know you are aware of him and are thinking of him. This is important when in the company of others, especially when it's your girlfriends! Husbands don't like to feel supplanted by their wife's friends.

N = *Nurture*

I like to make sure my busy husband feels nurtured by doing little, thoughtful things. I make sure his coffee is ready before he's out the door for his morning shift. He's a firefighter who gets up at 3:30 a.m. to commute to work. I make sure there is extra sharp white cheddar and a box of Triscuits for him to take to his shift. This is what he likes, so this is what he gets. Since he loves cheese so much, I have learned to make it for him myself. I've even attempted to make homemade crackers.

C = *Courage*

I find courage to learn new things rather than always relying on my husband, especially when he's feeling pressured. A helpless wife is not an asset! When something needs to be done, and he is too busy, I find a creative solution instead of complaining or nagging. It's a waste of time to badger him and serves as a bad example to the children. Keeping my mind sharp and active keeps my conversations interesting. I don't want my husband to become bored when we have time together. I want to fascinate him!

O = *Operate in the Spirit*

I need to be in constant communication with my Father in order to walk in love. I get my guidance, inspiration, and sense of purpose when I read the Word and pray throughout my day. If I don't live in the Spirit, I end up walking in my ugly ole' flesh. I start arguments, act grumpy, or get myself focused on "poor little me," which is a pity trip nobody in my family needs to live with.

I can't encourage my husband if I am discouraged myself. When I get my source of strength from God, I have fountains of living water. I can offer a drink to my thirsty husband and keep my children watered.

U = Utilize

I utilize what resources and gifts the Lord has given me. Nothing is as discouraging to a man as to hear his wife complain about all the things she's lacking. I want to be grateful, content, and happy. Proverbs 14:30 says, *"A sound heart is the life of the flesh: but envy the rottenness of the bones."*

R = Romance

A smart woman learns to like her husband as well as to love him. Make sure your husband knows you like him! Tell him. Cultivate loving feelings for him. Make time for dates. Encourage him in his dreams and pursuits. Why should he feel as if life is passing him by, while this ball and chain keeps him anchored and unhappy with demands and never-ending worries? I smile and wink in his direction once in awhile. I wear something pretty for him and try to stay healthy, in shape, and showered!

A = Affirm

Be enthusiastic about his ideas and plans. Be sure he knows you are rooting for him! Trust him to make wise decisions. Trust God when he doesn't. I have learned to pray instead of trying to change his mind. We discuss things of course, but I don't put him down! I don't brush off or criticize his ideas. I want to be his cheerleader. I try to bolster my husband's confidence before he goes out in the world. If you don't, there may be some sneaky, opportunistic woman out there, devoid of the Spirit of God, who might be willing to overlook those things that drive you crazy, and knows that men like to be admired and respected. Proverbs 18:14 says, *"The spirit of a man will sustain his infirmity; but a wounded spirit who can bear?"*

G = Grin

Smile. Laugh and be a fun person. I want to get as far away from a sour person as I can, as fast as I can! Proverbs 17:22 says, *"A merry heart doeth good like a medicine: but a broken spirit drieth the bones."* I try to keep a good sense of humor. It covers a multitude of sins!

E = Edit

Edit your thoughts and words. Keep them positive. Are you being kind? Appreciative? Encouraging? Thoughtful? I have a lot of selfish habits to eliminate, so I am on a mission to edit myself! I edit out anything that tears down my home and family. Proverbs 14:1 says, *"Every wise woman buildeth her house: but the foolish plucketh it down with her hands."*

DALYN WELLER
Yakima, Washington
dailywalkinfarm@yahoo.com

MY LIKES

I like to keep my husband's work car cleaned out every week—and smelling nice. Occasionally I put a treat and love note in the car. I also like to call him on the phone occasionally and say, "It's me!" Giggle. Then say, "I love you" really quickly. Giggle again! Then hang up the phone. He loves that! I like to make him a bedtime hot drink, rub his shoulders, and scratch his head with worship music softly playing.

JAIME CRAVEY

ASK YOUR HUSBAND

One day, pregnant with my first baby, I enjoyed tea with a Grandma friend in her immaculately kept kitchen. Drinking from a beautiful tea cup and smelling freshly baked goodies cooling, I asked her, "How do you get everything done? Your house is sparkling, and you look rested. I can't seem to get anything done, and I don't have any children yet!" Her reply is something I will never forget. She said, "Brandie, you have to start with one thing. That one thing is your husband." I was a little surprised. I mean, I knew how important it was to have a happy husband, but how does that translate to a clean house?

"Well," she continued, "when I was a young mother of three children, I had a hard time cleaning, although I always had dinner on the table when my husband got home. He always seemed to be irritated with me when he got home, like I hadn't done anything all day. He recognized that I was busy with three wee ones, but he was irked at the mess in the house. So I asked him, "What is one thing I can do to make you happier when you come home?'"

I expected him to say, "Clean the house!" But all he said was, "Can you clean off the coffee table? Everything else can be messy, but if the coffee table is clean, it makes me feel like I can come home, relax, and look at something nice and clean." Every day since them I have cleaned off the coffee table and made sure the glass was clean. He has been a happy camper ever since. I wasn't able to clean the house over night, but that was the first step. First, you make your priority to please your husband, then ASK him what he would like. You may be surprised. It may be easier than you thought."

I went home and asked my husband that night what one thing I could do for him. I had been very tired during the pregnancy and had been sleeping in when he went to work. He asked me to get up with him and make him breakfast and lunch. I did, even though it was difficult at first, and I found that I had more energy and time to do a bit more cleaning. The best part was that I had a happy husband who knew his wife cared and loved him enough to do what he really wanted in his heart.

That was 19 years and many children ago, and I still get up with him, even when pregnant and tired. I still have a hard time cleaning my house, homeschooling, and running after little "bitties" while being pregnant. But I know that my husband is satisfied, and *that* makes for a happy home, messy or clean.

BRANDI "BEE" LOGORIA

WORKING TOGETHER

With a large family of nine, I know my husband has concerns about trying to make a living and at the same time spending enough time with the family. It is hard for him to be away from home for long hours, knowing that certain projects need to be taken care of at home, too. I feel so fortunate to be able to stay home and school our children, make homemade meals and extra homemade goodies. When the weekend comes, knowing the extra work that needs to be done around the house, we all work together as a family. This is a special encouragement when we have to get ready for winter by filling our woodshed with LOTS of wood. It is much less stress for him throughout the week knowing that we will be ready to help with whatever needs to be done. Not only does the work get done more quickly, but we have time to have a fun event. Our favorite is a walk in the woods, along with a hot dog roast, and then listening to stories of daddy's childhood days in the very same woods.

RAE LYNN MIELKE
Marion Wisconsin, USA
raemar@frontiernet.net

SENSING HIS NEEDS

When I sense that my husband has had a rough day at work, physically or otherwise, I'll always suggest he hop in the shower right away so that I can give him a good massage! He rarely waits on that! If I hear him mention something during the course of the week that he'd like to eat, I'll be sure to fix it on Friday, so he can look forward to it. I'm trying to get better at this, but I do my best to prepare him very healthy meals.

One thing I KNOW that really encourages him is when I stick to our budget. When I show him some extra savings each month, he's really stoked! I try to make this my goal by cooking more from scratch and planning very simple, healthful meals.

However, the most encouraging thing my husband loves me to do is to show that I care for him—his dreams, goals, and concerns. I do this by conveying a sweet, loving, and supportive attitude, being on his team, lending support when he needs it, and seeing to my responsibilities as his wife.

DENISE BALIGAD
Wahiawa, Hawaii, USA
Pbaligad@aol.com

DADDY ALARM

At our house we have a "Daddy Alarm." This is a recurring alarm that I set on my cell phone. It goes off one hour before my husband arrives home from work. It reminds my children to clean up any messes around the house and tidy themselves up. It reminds the older children and me to start supper. It also reminds me to make sure my clothes are fresh, to fix my make-up and my hair, and to say a prayer for my big, sweet hubby.

To be honest, we are not as consistent with this as I would like to be. Sometimes the alarm goes off and I ignore it, thinking to myself that I'm "too busy." But when we are consistent, the results are not only a blessing to my husband, but a blessing to our whole household. My husband is never "too busy" to go to work to provide for his family, and this family should never be "too busy" to provide a warm, clean "Welcome Home" for him.

JULIE BANTON
Cerro Gordo, Illinois, USA
mothering9@yahoo.com

BE A WOMAN!

I've been married for over 30 years to one of the most wonderful men on the face of the earth. However, I didn't always encourage him. I always wanted to be encouraged MYSELF. I pitied myself for the all the hard work I was doing—raising children, cooking, cleaning house, homeschooling, and even teaching Sunday school, leading ladies groups, and lots of stuff I didn't need to be doing. I didn't think it was my job to *also* have to encourage my husband. But let me tell you, when I learned to do that, the blessings flowed in! We have so much more fun together. He's quick to help or pray over me when he sees that I'm overwhelmed. And he likes to take me on dates!

The following are some practical things I do to encourage him:

Respect him

I do not raise my voice, utter an ill word, criticize or complain about his ways or choices. If he's made a wrong choice, he's the one who will answer for it. As women, we are answerable to whether we submit to our husbands, not to whether our husbands made good choices or decisions that we liked.

Admire him

When he's out working (my husband is a pastor, but also works fulltime here on our honeybee farm), I make it a point to go out and see what he's doing. I even ask him to explain what he's doing. He loves it! I'll sometimes crawl up under the car or up on a roof so he can explain the work he's doing. It doesn't matter if I don't understand it; what matters is that I care enough about *him* that I want to know what he's doing.

When he brings home his paycheck I say, "Hallelujah! Great job!" I say this even if he's brought home the same paycheck week after week after week for years. When he's faced with a troubling situation, I tell him, "Go get 'em. You can handle that. It's a piece of cake!"

Help him

As his helpmeet, I ask him frequently if there is anything he needs, or if I can get anything for him. If he's at the other end of the farm, I ride my bike or drive the jeep down to check on him and see if there's anything he needs. It's not at all unusual for him to be working with the honeybees and realize he's in need of something. He knows if he only waits, I will be out to check and go get him whatever he needs.

Provide a cozy castle for him

I refuse to let anyone or anything disrupt our home environment—whether it's unruly children, neighbors, friends, people from church, bills, problems, or the phone. We have a saying in our house that "the world gets bad past the mailbox." When my husband walks in the door, things are calm, soothing, and peaceful. The house is inviting, clutter-free, and the children are in their place. There's a fire in the fireplace, candles (pure beeswax, of course!) are burning, and a wonderful meal is ready for him on the table. This tells him, "We want you here and love you to be here." And he wants to be!

Be a woman to him

There's nothing more encouraging to a man than having a woman who wants to be a woman and treat her man right! So often we get caught up in so much baby-stuff, toddler games, school work, and day-to-day life that we forget we are a woman and fail to treat our husbands like a lover. If necessary, "wash" the day off with a nice warm shower, put on something he likes, and go treat him good!

SHERI BURNS
Fairmount, Illinois, USA
sheri@tswireless.net

MAKE THE WEEKENDS SPECIAL

My husband, Jeff, works long hours during the week, so I try to make his weekends worthy of "bragging rights" at his work on Monday morning. I make sure he sleeps in while I wake up early with our toddler and make him a special breakfast. The morning and afternoon is his to enjoy. Whatever he wants to do is what we do. And I do it joyfully. What Jeff wants to do is not always the most fun, like digging trenches, spreading compost, or going to the comic book shop. But I do it without complaint and with a smile. On a recent weekend, we met our family at the cider mill and picked apples. On the Sunday we took a long motorcycle ride after church.

When Jeff says to me, "I wish I had more time, I would love to do this..." I make a mental note and make it happen. Making the weekends special for Jeff often means a lot of work for me, but when he leaves for his job on Monday morning and says, "Amber,

I'm going to miss you. I didn't want the weekend to end," it is worth every sacrifice.

AMBER ARNOLD
Casco Twp, Michigan, USA
amberjanicki@yahoo.com

SURPRISE BIRTHDAY

My husband, Karl, had been going through a difficult time around his birthday. I got an idea. I gave him a card for his birthday, asking him out to supper. During the day I packed everything we needed for camping. I packed fun treats, his favorite game, and a book to read together. Some friends went to a camp ground and set up their camper for us to stay in. That evening we dropped our son off at grandpa and grandma's, my husband thinking we were just going out for supper. After supper I gave my husband another card inviting him to spend the weekend with me. He was completely surprised! It was a blessing to have time together and to be able to enjoy some time away without expensive hotel costs!

SARAH SNEATH
Salina, Kansas, USA
krawlandsarey@gmail.com

TOP TEN

The following are my "top ten" list of things I like to do to encourage my husband:

1. When he is traveling, I sneak a card or love note into his suitcase.
2. When he is taking a sack lunch to work I have made for him, I put in a picture that the children drew especially for him.

3. On a workday when he has something especially tough ahead, I leave an encouraging note on the dashboard of his car.
4. In the morning I make his coffee and breakfast.
5. I sneak a peek at his "To Do" list and find things I can do for him.
6. When he leaves the house, the children and I all huddle around the front window and wave goodbye to him as he drives away, waving to him the American Sign Language "I love you" sign and yelling loud enough to wake all the neighbors up, "Bye, we love you!"
7. I call him at work every day at noon to check in, say "I love you," and ask him if there is anything he needs me to do. I've done this so consistently for the past nine years that he gets concerned if I happen to be a little late in calling.
8. I regularly thank him for being such a good provider and for working hard so that I can stay home with the children. I also tell him what a great father he is and point out when his fathering skills are especially good in a certain area.
9. When he comes from work, my goal is to greet him with the five senses. This is what I *try* to do:
   Sight: When he comes through the door, I have the house, the children and myself looking presentable.
   Touch: When he comes through the door, I greet him with warm hugs, kisses and maybe even a little back rub!
   Sound: When he comes through the door...
   ♥ I do not talk on the phone. Everyone I speak with regularly on the phone knows that when I hear my husband driving up the driveway, the phone call ends.
   ♥ I have the television off (unless it is his Monday night football game).
   ♥ I allow no whining, crying, or screaming children.
   ♥ I save my need to speak with him about all the issues of the day until later, and greet him only with words of blessing and "I'm so glad your home."

♥ Sometimes I have some of his favorite relaxing music playing--praise music, jazz, or other soothing music.

Smell: My husband loves to have dinner ready when he walks in the door. The smell of food cooking is so comforting.

Taste: If dinner is not ready, I have a little plate of appetizers for him to munch on while he waits, such as cheese and crackers, chips and salsa, etc.

10.   I pray diligently for him.

GINA CALLAGHAN
Walnut Creek, California, USA
gina.ed@sbcglobal.net

MISSION ACCOMPLISHED

My husband is an expert at many trades. Because he has so many talents, people constantly call him for help on their projects or when they have emergencies. My husband has a mentally demanding job, plus he is in the process of remodeling our third home. He carries the "weight of the world" on his shoulders and yet is still a great dad and husband.

When he turned thirty, I planned a wonderful birthday celebration to show him how much we cherished him, but at the last minute he had to go out of town for two weeks. I was very disappointed, but instead of sulking, I decided to get creative. Before he left, we had huge fir trees trimmed in our front and back yard. The debris was at least three feet high and covered most of our front yard and a huge chunk of our back yard. He actually hauled away three truck loads previously and it did not even make a dent in the piles.

For his birthday, I made flyers with his picture on it and staged a "WORK PARTY" for him. "Come with gloves and a happy heart! Refreshments and pizza will be served." I advertised. On the exact day of his birthday, a group of people sweated up a storm and removed the piles. It actually took a couple of days to finish it all. The volunteers were so excited for Clinton to come home to a clean lawn that they came back the second day to finish. In between all the brush removal, I caulked and painted some new siding that he put up months before and repainted the front door, fireplace and entry bench. I even landscaped a small part of the yard that was torn up while remodeling. He thought I paid a tree removal service to clean up the property, but when I told him what happened, was he in love with me! Mission accomplished!

EMMA SARA MCMILLAN
Brookings, Oregon, USA
mcmillan4him@yahoo.com

HE'S MY PRIORITY

The following are my ideas to encourage my husband:

Pray for him daily

This should be first and foremost as we have no idea what our husbands face on the job every day. I pray over my husband with the children at least twice daily, at breakfast and lunch as we say grace. We pray for his protection, strength, and for a good day for him. Also in my devotion time, I pray that the Lord will continually strengthen him spiritually and that I will be the helpmeet to my husband that I should be on a daily basis.

Verbally express your love to him

"Your man" is desperate to know how much he is loved by you and the children. Encourage your children to show their daddy they love him. After 10 long hard hours of working tactile stimulation, there is nothing like coming home to hugging, holding, smooching, and massaging!

Write uplifting notes to him

Write your favorite, uplifting Bible passages or loving little notes from "Your Baby" or pet name he calls you and place them where your husband will see them when he gets up in the morning, or maybe when he comes home, tired and needing a boost!

Spend time with him

When the children are in bed, sit next to him and let him share his thoughts and concerns with you while you quietly listen. Then maybe you can both pray together over them. Praying together always draws couples closer to the Lord and to each other. My husband and I sit and read books together, which lets him know I enjoy being with him.

Serve him

This may mean putting his needs above yours or the children's. He needs to know by your actions that he comes first, whether at the dinner table or in conversations. Your children are very important, but they will not always live with you. You will live with your husband until death parts you.

Respect him

Serving is a form of respect. Your husband is your God-given authority and protection over you. We must not take this lightly. If we want our children to respect their fathers, then as their mothers we must give them a very good example to follow. When my husband asks me to come, for whatever reason, I drop what I am doing and go immediately. I do not make any major, and very few minor decisions, without first speaking to my husband to let him make to final decision.

LORI

THE "BLESSINGS" LIST

Growing up my mother ALWAYS mowed the lawn. I don't think I ever saw my dad mow the law. He would go out after Mom was done and do all the detail work and set up the sprinklers to water (automatic sprinklers—what was THAT?). But it was always Momma out there mowing.

I never thought anything about it until I met my husband. "Mowing is MAN'S work," he stated emphatically. He made it sound so wonderful that there were just certain things a man was to do for his woman and that my mother should not have to mow the lawn. So when we got married, one of hubby's responsibilities was to mow the lawn. I loved the fact that I was cared for in such a special way. I started to create "honey do" lists for my husband. After all, there were jobs for women and jobs for men. But I realized that my "honey do" list was getting longer and longer and nothing was being done. And once children entered the picture, I noticed the lawn was rarely getting done as well. And when the lawn WAS getting done, family time with Daddy was not.

I realized that my husband's workweek (usually 80 hours or more) takes him away from his family. He really wants to spend time with the children and myself. And he would rather do that than mow the lawn or anything on my "honey do" list. So rather than add to the list, I am starting to cross things off. Not because I don't want/need them done anymore, but because I am doing them. I have finally gotten over the whole "that is something for a man to do" attitude (which was really weighing my husband down because I was adding so much to the list for him to do). Instead, I have the "blessings" list. If my hubby has the time and wants to do it, what a blessing it is to me! If he doesn't and I do it, it becomes a blessing to him, by allowing him to spend the precious little time he has with us and not feel guilty about not doing something else that I added to the list.

This afternoon, while the girls were playing quietly on the deck and baby was sleeping, I went out and mowed the lawn for the first time. It felt great! This weekend, rather than my husband feeling guilty the lawn is not mowed (he wants to go to a museum the girls have asked to go to), he can enjoy the whole weekend with us going through the museum and seeing the awe and wonder on the girls' faces. He can explain things to them and feel satisfaction in teaching them. I am so thankful that I changed my "honey do" list into a "blessings" list.

PAULA GIPSON
Colorado Springs, Colorado, USA
plgipson@earthlink.net

FILL UP TO POUR OUT

I can only encourage my husband and children when I'm encouraged. I believe it's so important for me to daily encourage myself in the Lord by spending quality time with God. Then I am able to:

1. Encourage my husband by initiating fun times. It's not always my husband's job to initiate these things. Often he's tired, too. Too often we wives wait to be served instead of initiating.

2. Encourage my husband by giving him a hug in the course of the day or evening.

3. Encourage my husband by taking time to have coffee break in the middle of the afternoon or evening, especially when I have fresh baked goods. He enjoys the fact that I take time to sit down and talk to him, or just sit together. It's also a great confidence builder for the children to see us do this together.

4. Encourage my husband by giving him space to spend time with God, or to just sit and think or do something he finds relaxing. I think a husband can very easily feel overwhelmed when he comes home from work and all he sees is more work and responsibilities. He needs to know that there are times when he can come home and just relax and enjoy his family. It's my responsibility to be sensitive and create such an atmosphere for him when the need arises.

TINA WIEBE
Straffordville, Ontario, Canada
htwiebe@amtelecom.net

A WIDOW SPEAKS OUT

My husband of 29 years suddenly and unexpectedly went home to be with the Lord. My husband had taken our children, 13 and 9, for a fun day at the amusement park and had a heart attack while waiting in line for the next rollercoaster ride.

Randy and I read many books and attended numerous marriage seminars through the years. However, I have learned more about marriage in my short time as a widow than I ever did as a wife. It has reinforced the priorities I already knew were essential. As a widow, I would encourage you to:

1. Live each day with your husband as if it were your last day together.
2. Don't let the daily trials and disappointments of life determine your steps.
3. Let the Lord lead you and listen intently to His voice as He prompts you to love and minister to your husband.
4. Let your husband be who he is and let the Lord order his steps. I think we spend too much time trying to determine who our husband should be and how he should serve the Lord. Instead, we should support and love him as Jesus does, with all his strengths and weaknesses.
5. Let him see the joy of the Lord on your face and a genuine look of acceptance and love for him. Let him see the Lord's light shining through you. Let him know that you love him.
6. Do not stand behind or in front of him, but come alongside him. Walk together as you navigate your way through life.
7. "Don't sweat the small stuff." When you have discord, resolve it quickly and don't give the enemy a stronghold. Sometimes it is better to be kind than to be right.
8. Forgive him as Christ has forgiven you.

CAROLYN LOWE
Schertz, Texas, USA
calowe@sbcglobal.net

LOVE IS A VERB

What does it mean to love someone? We have all heard these words hundreds of times. Romantic novelists tell us that love is a whirlwind of shared joy and happiness intermingled with hearty doses of nights out on the town, candle-lit dinners for two and heart-pounding love letters. Psychologists tell us that to love someone is to spend "quality" time together and "communicate."

All these things are good, and surely couples who practice them have experienced a better relationship. But what if you are unequally yoked to an unbeliever? What if your spouse doesn't act lovingly toward you? What if now that the Lord is blessing you with children, you can't afford to, or have little energy left to pursue the fun dating activities that originally brought you together? Sadly, when faced with these types of growing pains, many couples feel as though they have "fallen out of love" and seek a separation and ultimately divorce.

God looks at love differently. Biblical love is a verb, a word that indicates action; not a noun which would indicate, as the world implores, a feeling.

Many married couples in Biblical times did not even know each other before marriage. Isaac and Rebekah, for example, lived many miles from each other. Moses and Zipporah, and Jacob and Leah were not even drawn together by a common bond or goal. Therefore, when Paul beseeched husbands and wives to love each other, he was not encouraging them to ignite the old flame through whirlwind nights on the town. He was, instead, encouraging them to love as an action. In 1Corinthians 13, God gives us a look at love by His standards.

Love is patient—even when you feel like forcefully expressing yourself.

Love is kind—even when your husband is not nice to you, and you really want to retaliate.

Love is not jealous—especially when hubby comes home too tired to listen after giving all of his energy and time to work, and you feel you are going unnoticed.

Love does not brag—even when you want to tell the world about your accomplishments.

Love is not arrogant—but is humble, assuming others to be right when they correct us.

Love does not act unbecomingly—even when being rude and overbearing would allow you to get your way.

Love does not seek her own—even when it would seem profitable for you to do so.

Love is not easily provoked—even when you've been changing dirty diapers all day, and your husband comes home irritated from a long day at work.

Love does not take into account a wrong suffered—even when it seems everyone is against you or demeaning you for following Christ or allowing God to plan your family.

Love does not rejoice in unrighteousness—even when it seems that the other person deserved the ill treatment.

Love rejoices with the truth—even when it seems easier to lie or mislead.

Love bears all things—even when disappointments seem overwhelming.

Love believes all things—even when you've been hurt and don't feel like trusting your husband or anyone any more.

Love hopes all things—even though your visions have been dimmed by years of disappointments

Love endures all things—especially when you think you can't endure the people or the circumstances in your life anymore.

Love never fails—even when you feel overwhelmed and your situation seems hopeless.

Love will not crumble when placed in stressful or difficult situations, but instead remains selflessly faithful even to the point of death.

ANGELA DECOTEAU
St. Amant, Louisiana, USA
decotec@eatel.net

Chapter 14

WHAT DO HUSBANDS SAY?

Some time ago I did a survey asking husbands in many different states what qualities they honored in their wives. We may "think" we know what husbands like, but I am sure the best idea is to hear directly from them. The following are some of their answers, which were reiterated again and again.

- I honor her because I can count on her. I can trust her completely.
- I honor her because of her love and devotion to God and to the family.
- I love the way she thinks about the needs of our family and of others before herself.
- I honor her for her submissive spirit to me, which I don't demand of her, but which she willingly gives to me.
- I honor her because she acknowledges me as the head of our home, rather than making the decisions herself.
- I honor her when I see her seeking after God to be a virtuous woman.
- I honor her as the keeper of our home.
- I honor her as she bears our children and ministers to the family and to the needs of others.
- I respect her for completing me. She "catches my slack." She is a wonderful nurturer and tends our nest. I have to work and provide, but coming home is what I really look forward to.
- I respect her softness and tenderness. She softens me and at the same time lets me be a tough guy.
- I honor her because she lets me lead.
- I honor her because she forgives me, even when I do the same dumb things over and over and over and over again.
- I honor her because she is feminine and gracious.

We observe from the above statements that men honor and respect a woman who embraces all that God created her to be—a tender nurturer and mother, a woman with a "gentle" spirit who lets her man take his leadership and be a real man as God created him to be. One of the greatest ways to keep our marriage strong is not to compete for our husband's role, but to embrace our own role, the divine mandate God has given us—femininity, womanliness, conception, wombing, mothering, nurturing, nourishing, nesting, succoring, enriching, encouraging, helping, inspiring, comforting, and self-sacrificing for our husbands and our families.

NANCY CAMPBELL

- Chapter 15 -

YOUR OWN IDEAS

I am sure wonderful things have been happening in your marriage as you have encouraged your husband by the many ideas in this book. But there are many more ways. As you think of new ideas, write them down on this page.

Made in the USA
Charleston, SC
30 April 2011